DISCARDED

W9-DIJ-486

The Merrill Studies
in
Paterson

Compiled by

John Engels

St. Michael's College

We are pleased to send you this book for
your review purposes.   The book was
published   in 1971
and is priced: ~~clothbound~~xxxxxxxxxxxxx
                        paperback $1.75
Please send copy of review.
CHARLES E. MERRILL PUBLISHING CO.
Columbus, Ohio   43216

Charles E. Merrill Publishing Company
A Bell & Howell Company
Columbus, Ohio

DISCARDED

CHARLES E. MERRILL STUDIES

Under the General Editorship of
Matthew J. Bruccoli and Joseph Katz

Copyright © 1971 by Charles E. Merrill Publishing Company, Columbus, Ohio. All rights reserved. No part of this book may be reproduced
in any form, electronic or mechanical, including photocopy, recording,
or any information storage and retrieval system without permission in
writing from the publisher.

ISBN: 0–675–09212–4

Library of Congress Catalog Number: 79–150077

1 2 3 4 5 6 7 8 9 10—79 78 77 76 75 74 73 72 71

Printed in the United States of America

Florida Gulf Coast University

Preface

Paterson is not an easy poem to read, being untidy, packed, bulging and bristling with the plenitude of contraries that add up to a city, a rather indiscriminately selected lot of things, it appears at first glance, and sometimes at second, and scarcely organized in the usual ways.

It is a poem through which, as Edwin Honig says, one may "walk or fly or stagger a dozen times," proceeding each time "in a different way," and emerging "each time with a different set of meanings, a different sense of the fusion of the parts, and a different feeling of exaltation and exasperation." It is that way in life, too, and it is sometimes the case in *Paterson,* as in life, that exasperation gets the upper hand. It is one purpose of this book to help avoid that.

Another is to provide an accessible body of critical opinion, which will pay attention to at least a few of the "hundreds of things in the poem," as Randall Jarrell says, "that deserve specific mention." A further aim is to acquaint the reader of *Paterson* with some of the basic critical questions to which this poem continues to give rise; and, finally —because all of the ordinary logical and dramatic transitions seem to be missing, the poet plunging around with his nose into everything, sometimes into everything all at once, and the reader in desperate need of a critical bearing—this book hopes to provide a station whereon the reader may enjoy an initial, if merely temporary, stability of perspective.

Since Book One of *Paterson* appeared in 1946 there has been a small, now growing, body of criticism dealing specifically with the poem. Many of the first critical attempts were tentative, often baffled, usually brief. They were given over either to general, subjective commentary, or to dogged efforts towards imposing order, to tidying things up; the poem constitutes, after all, a grievous affront to anyone irritated by the trackless, or by literary Irish pennants. And as the poem continued to grow beyond anyone's expectation, critical bewilderment and excitement kept pace.

But only recently have any really successful efforts been made to see the poem in the contexts and traditions of American poetry and in the light of the whole body of Williams' work. And only recently has it become to any degree evident how much of an influence *Paterson* has been on the younger American poets, constituting, perhaps, a formal and thematic matrix for all the best work done since the fifties. The differences between the earlier, shorter poems and the immensely long, architectural, allusive, and symbolically organized *Paterson* are no longer seen as formal discrepancies, but as parts of one aesthetic impulse, antedating even *In the American Grain,* to define the American locale, to "return to the ground."

Williams' place in the American literary tradition as rebel, iconoclast, formal theorist and innovator and, paradoxically, sometime conventional practitioner; his role as breaker and remolder; his work as informing and containing in perhaps higher degree than that of any other American poet those energies of vision and imagination most peculiarly American—these are the primary subjects of critical examination today.

This book contains critical essays and reviews both early and contemporary; and while they provide glosses on the poem, they may incidentally give a partial view of the nature of the critical development centering on the work of an important American epic poet.

This collection cannot be complete; it is, in fact, a wholly arbitrary collection, as any such critical anthology must be. By the time this book is in print, I expect that many new discussions of the poem will have come out in the quarterlies; and it might be well to point out here that it was not possible to reprint some articles which, had more room been available, would certainly be included in this book. John Thirlwall's essay in *New Directions in Prose and Poetry 17,* which makes use of much of the material in the Buffalo and Yale collections, was simply too long to print, but is essential reading.

Again, while I had intended to include the equally essential preface to Walter Scott Peterson's *An Approach to Paterson* (Yale University Press, 1967) it so closely interlocks with the rest of that book, and devotes so much space to a preliminary discussion of *In the American Grain,* that the required editing would have been a disservice to the essay.

Joel O. Conarroe's "The Preface to *Paterson*" which appeared in *Contemporary Literature* (Winter 1969) is an important critical commentary, but cannot be reprinted at this time; nor was it possible to obtain editorial permission to reprint Hugh Kenner's "With the Bare Hands," an early long review-article which first appeared in *Poetry* (August 1952) and later in Mr. Kenner's *Gnomon* (Ivan Obolensky, Inc., 1958). I regret this omission. Louis Martz's "The Unicorn In *Paterson*" has been anthologized elsewhere, and space limitations precluded the use of his discussion of *Paterson* in *The Poem of the Mind* (Oxford University Press, 1966). "The Unicorn in *Paterson*" remains so far the best commentary on Book Five of the poem, but I have chose—again arbitrarily—to use only material not previously reprinted.

Contents

1. Contemporary Reviews

2. Essays

Contents

1. Contemporary Reviews

Edwin Honig

The City of Man

Through *Paterson* (*Book I*) one may walk or fly or stagger a dozen times—one proceeds in a different way at each reading of the poem—and emerge each time with a different set of meanings, a different sense of the fusion of the parts, and a different feeling of exaltation and exasperation.

As the first unit of a long philosophic poem, it calls for a special kind of attention and evaluation. Though published in book form, it obviously cannot be treated as any other book of verse which does not similarly point to a still unpublished and larger design. One must also dodge the momentarily fruitless question of its unity or fragmentariness as a part in order to determine first what the poet promises and what the poem itself suggests of purpose and direction. Then, because the promises, like those of the magician, are but the invitations to suspend belief, which is swept up in the miracle of performance, it might better serve to show how the incredible richness of the poet's effects exalts by mystification and exasperates by seeming deception.

Williams proposes to prove "that a man in himself is a city, beginning, seeking, achieving and concluding his life in ways which the various aspects of a city may embody—if imaginatively conceived—any city, all the details of which may be made to voice his most intimate convictions." Thus a man may become a treasury, a legend taking unto himself all the proportions of a city, historical and contemporary, animate and inanimate, moribund and waking. The city becomes the focal myth wound out of the poet's consciousness, or, like the dreams of the hero of *Finnegans Wake*, the myth becomes the consciousness itself.

But what of the philosophy, the poetic logic, the use of guiding symbol, referents, central images, and artifice to bind the whole together? These do not appear according to any conventional pattern. The events of history themselves—with which the poet interlards his verse: letters from friends, snatches from old newspapers, archival records, the documents of past and present—

Reprinted, with changes by the author, from *Poetry,* LXIX (February 1947), 277–84, copyright 1947 by the Modern Poetry Association. Reprinted by permission of the Editor of *Poetry* and Edwin Honig.

provide the links, the scattered facts which the broad imaginative conception seeks to co-ordinate. Tentatively, however, some such rough scheme may be delineated: for the philosophy: "no ideas but in things"; for the poetic logic: "to make a start,/ out of particulars/ and make them general"; for the guiding symbol: man as a city; for the referents: (what Williams has said in another place) "my sources . . ./the secret of that form/interknit with the unfathomable ground/where we walk daily"; for the central images: the river, the falls, the rocks, the green things separately growing; and for the artifice: a language, to use Williams' quote from J. A. Symonds, of "deformed verse . . . suited to deformed morality."

Like any long-festering preoccupation with life which erupts into art, the poem is both a personal confession and a challenge to the forces which besiege the poet's creative faith. In a life which proves only that "we know nothing, pure/and simple, beyond/our own complexities,"

> . . . The how (the howl) only
> is at my disposal (proposal) : watching—
> colder than stone.
> A bud forever green,
> tight-curled upon the pavement, perfect
> in juice and substance but divorced, divorced
> from its fellows, fallen low—
> Divorce is
> the sign of knowledge in our time,
> divorce! divorce!

As with another "divorced" contemporary, T. S. Eliot (whose resolution may be clearer because his faith is orthodox, though his knowledge is no fuller), the personal problem with Williams is to discover and constantly rediscover a language which will embody the forms of fluxive reality. Eliot seeks the language fitting the imagination to God; Williams, the language fitting the imagination to things. For Williams it is not the language of the university, of the scholarly "non-purveyors," "the knowledgeable idiots" who restrict knowledge, but of one who feels like the branch of a sycamore, trembling

> among the rest, separate, slowly
> with giraffish awkwardness, slightly
> on a long axis, so slightly
> as hardly to be noticed, in itself the tempest. . . .

who would rescue something of the waste of moment-to-moment
reality:

> The sun
>   winding the yellow bindweed about a
>   bush; worms and gnats, life under a stone.
>   The pitiful snake with its mosaic skin
>   and frantic tongue. The horse, the bull
>   the whole din of fracturing thought
>   as it falls tinnily to nothing upon the streets
>   and the absurd dignity of a locomotive
>   hauling freight—

He would believe in "The vague inaccuracy of events dancing
two/ and two with language which they/ forever surpass," and
would seem to demand that his own crotchety choice of quotations be judged, however faulty their language, as records of
that reality embedded in events which the poet at best only occasionally grasps in his own verse.

They are his proof of an ever-present and ever-past activity
of spirit which has penetrated the inanimate world: the senti-
mentality with which the knowledge of the prior penetration
there by others inverts the scene, *e.g.*, the heroic and pathetic
deaths of those in the past which make the waterfalls over the
river legendary, and the perverse assumption of some accredited
accomplishment in the obscure persons and events which reenact
the poet's sense of wonder in the place, forever absorbed and
rejected as he is by his environment. Obsessed with the sources
of things, and with the mystic's proprietary rights, he seeks to
maintain the balance between sheer surface illusion and sharp
plunging insight into their being. Although at times admitting with
others his failure to find what "laughs at the names/by which they
think to trap it. Escapes!/ Never by running but by lying still,"
he is often rewarded by the scrupulous intensity of his vision with
lines like

> And the air lying over the water
> lifts the ripples, brother
> to brother, touching as the mind touches,
> counter-current. . . .
>   brings in the rumors of separate
> worlds, the birds as against the fish, the grape
> to the green weed that streams out undulant . . .

Pointing to the harmony that must be created out of the eternal
sense of the duplicity in things, the poet, doctor-like, with skill
and passion, and without cheating himself, affirms his power to
control the flux by defining and ministering to it.

Williams' verses insist on themselves, insist on their own self-
distractedness, their own "deformity"; they insist on their own
explosions from sense and their own sure bringing together of the
strands of sense, like music more than verse, like fluid water color,
trembling with motion while at rest, themselves part of all motion
when motion momently, quixotically freezes into rest.

Book I, which "introduces the elemental character of the place,"
thereby also introduces the poet's magical paraphernalia, his
reiterative symbols, his episodic devices, the links in his Man-
City chain. Several readings will ostensibly justify the growing
magnitude of poetic conception. But though one is willing to
applaud the achievement, it becomes increasingly difficult to
validate as integral parts of the poetry the successive chunks
of prose interlardings, which one instinctively wants to skip on
rereading the poem. And one is made conscious of the faltering
gestures of objective relationship between the poet and his human
surroundings. His love of the human is fixed, alien, and cold, a
pity self-magnified; yet he persists in that identification as an almost classic necessity. The reason is perhaps not far to find.
It is not love of the human, but a recognition in their actions of
the forces in men by which they try to extend themselves, their
fumbling illiterate use of the language of sex ("an incredible/
clumsiness of address,/senseless rapes"), of imagination (Sam
Patch, the inspired professional jumper, who at last failed because
he had *lost words*), curiosity and knowledge, forces which wealth
and poverty cut short and divorce from living. Facing people, the
poet confronts the complicated equations of their lives, "con-
trolled" but unmanageable. Wishing to embrace in order to sustain
them, like the City, he finds that the problem resolves itself into a
personal "mathematic."

> The thought returns: Why have I not
> but for imagined beauty where there is none
> or none available, long since
> put myself deliberately in the way of death?

Make the pathetic leap? End up in the river frozen in an ice cake,
"incommunicado"? But he has only lately discovered his voice,

> Only of late, late! begun to know, to
> know clearly (as through clear ice) whence
> I draw my breath or how to employ it
> clearly—if not well. . . .

And through the lover who sits by the bank of the river at the side of his beloved, proposing

> to pass beyond
> the moment of meeting, while the
> currents float still in mid-air, to
> fall—
> with you from the brink, before
> the crash—
> to seize the moment.

—the poet comes to know the language which failed the others, which fails the people who "have not the courage" to use it. This sense of discovery is extremely personal, welding together as it does the poetic esthetic with a criticism of man which subsumes the poet's very acceptance of the living condition. It accounts for the marvel of the poet's recreation of things through a consciousness inbred with the underlying shifts of nature. But it does not reconcile that sense with any sense of solution of the "problem of language" in man.

If the City is ultimately made to embody the Man, it will be because the time and events which identify the place have been surpassed by the universality toward which the Man-as-City strives. Though possibly violating Williams' conception and effectively bypassing the inconclusiveness of the objective human relationship, this statement may perhaps explain the insistent power of the poetry. For when all the apparatus which has been created to implement it has faded from the design, the mystery of the poet's creation remains, as in the last lines, an attainment of personal faith: the reawakened knowledge that only through a penetration to the sources of being, the active acknowledgment of primitive earth forces, does life, the language of thought and action, become real or intelligible:

> Thought clambers up
> snail like, upon the wet rocks
> hidden from sun and sight—
> hedged in by the pouring torrent—

and has its birth and death there
in that moist chamber, shut from
the world—and unknown to the world,
cloaks itself in mystery— . . .

Robert Lowell

Paterson II

"Paterson," Book Two, is an interior monologue. A man spends
Sunday in the park at Paterson, New Jersey. He thinks and look
about him; his mind contemplates, describes, comments, associates,
stops, stutters, and shifts like a firefly, bound only by its milieu.
The man is Williams, anyone living in Paterson, the American, the
masculine principle—a sort of Everyman. His monologue is interrupted by chunks of prose: paragraphs from old newspapers, text-
books, and the letters of a lacerated and lacerating poetess. This
material is merely selected by the author. That the poetry is able
to digest it in the raw is a measure of power and daring—the daring of simplicity; for only a taut style with worlds of experience
behind it could so resign, and give way to the anthologist. The
didactic chapters in "Moby Dick" have a similar function, and are
the rock that supports the struggles of Captain Ahab.

The park is Everywoman, any woman, the feminine principle,
America. The water roaring down the falls from the park to Paterson is the principle of life. The rock is death, negation, the *nul;*
carved and given form, it stands for the imagination, "like a red
basalt grasshopper, boot-long with window-eyes." The symbols are
not allegorical, but loose, intuitive, and Protean.

"Paterson," like Hart Crane's "Marriage of Faustus and Helen,"
is about marriage. "Rigor of beauty is the quest." Everything in
the poem is masculine or feminine, everything strains toward marriage, but the marriages never come off, except in the imagination,

Reprinted from *The Nation,* CLXVI (June 19, 1948), 692–94, by permission
of *The Nation.*

and there, attenuated, fragmentary, and uncertain. "Divorce is
the sign of knowledge in our time." The people "reflect no beauty
but gross ... unless it is beauty to be, anywhere, so flagrant in
desire." "The ugly legs of the young girls, pistons without deli-
cacy"; "not undignified"; "among the working classes *some* sort
of breakdown has occurred." The preacher in the second section,
attended by the "iron smiles" of his three middle-aged disciples,
by "benches on which a few children have been propped by the
others against their running off," "bends at the knees and straight-
ens himself up violently with the force of his emphasis—like
Beethoven getting a crescendo out of an orchestra"—ineffective,
pathetic, and a little phony. He has given up, or says he has given
up, a fortune for the infinite riches of our Lord Jesus Christ. Interspersed through his sermon, as an ironic counter-theme, is Alex-
ander Hamilton, whose fertile imagination devised the national
debt and envisioned Paterson as a great manufacturing center.
Nobody wins. "The church spires still spend their wits against the
sky." "The rock-table is scratched by the picnickers' boot-nails,
more than by the glacier." The great industrialists are "those
guilty bastards ... trying to undermine us." The legislators are
"under the garbage, uninstructed, incapable of self-instruction."
"An orchestral dulness overlays their world." "The language,
tongue-tied ... words without style!"

This is the harsh view. Against it is the humorous, the dogs, the
children; lovely fragments of natural description; the author's
sense of the human and sympathetic in his people.

Williams is noted as an imagist, a photographic eye; in Book
One he has written "no ideas but in the facts." This is misleading.
His symbolic man and woman are Hegel's *thesis* and *antithesis*.
They struggle toward *synthesis*—marriage. But fulness, if it exists
at all, only exists in simple things, trees and animals; so Williams,
like other Platonists, is thrown back on the "idea." "And no whiteness (lost) is so white as the memory of whiteness." "The stone
lives, the flesh dies." The idea, Beauty, must be realized by the
poet where he lives, in Paterson. "Be reconciled, Poet, with your
world, it is the only truth," though "love" for it "is no comforter,
rather a nail in the skull."

"Paterson" is an attempt to write the American Poem. It depends on the American myth, a myth that is seldom absent from
our literature—part of our power, and part of our hubris and deformity. At its grossest the myth is propaganda, puffing and
grimacing: Size, Strength, Vitality, the Common Man, the New

World, Vital Speech, the Machine; the hideous neo-Roman personae: Democracy, Freedom, Liberty, the Corn, the Land. How hollow, windy, and inert this would have seemed to an imaginative man of another culture! But the myth is a serious matter. It is assumed by Emerson, Whitman, and Hart Crane; by Henry Adams and Henry James. For good or for evil, America *is* something immense, crass, and Roman. We must unavoidably place ourselves in our geography, history, civilization, institutions, and future.

The subjects of great poetry have usually been characters and the passions, a moral struggle that calls a man's whole person into play. One thinks of the wrath of Achilles, Macbeth and his conscience, Aeneas debating whether he will leave Dido, whether he will kill Turnus. But in the best long American poems—"Leaves of Grass," "The Cantoes," "The Waste Land," "Four Quartets," "The Bridge," and "Paterson"—no characters take on sufficient form to arrive at a crisis. The people melt into voices. In a recent essay Eliot has given his reasons why a writer should, perhaps, read Milton; Williams has answered with an essay that gives reasons why a writer should *not* read Milton—Eliot and Williams might learn something from "Paradise Lost" and "Samson Agonistes," how Milton populated his desert.

Until Books III and IV are published, it is safer to compare "Paterson" with poems that resemble it; not with "The Bridge," that wonderful monster, so unequal, so inexperienced—dazzling in its rhetoric at times in the way that Keats is dazzling; but with a book in which its admirers profess to find everything, "Leaves of Grass." Whitman is a considerable poet, and a considerable myth. I can never quite disentangle the one from the other. I would say that Whitman's language has less variety, sureness, and nerve than Williams's; that his imagination is relatively soft, formless, monotonous, and vague. Both poets are strong on compassion and enthusiasm, but these qualities in Whitman are *simpliste* and blurred.

"Paterson" is Whitman's America, grown pathetic and tragic, brutalized by inequality, disorganized by industrial chaos, and faced with annihilation. No poet has written of it with such a combination of brilliance, sympathy, and experience, with such alertness and energy. Because he has tried to understand rather than excoriate, and because in his maturity he has been occupied with the "raw" and the universal, his "Paterson" is not the tragedy of the outcast but the tragedy of our civilization. It is a book in which the best readers, as well as the simple reader, are likely to find *everything*.

Edwin Honig

The "Paterson" Impasse

In Book Two of *Paterson*, Dr. Williams' long poem-in-progress, the character of the work as testament and confession becomes more pronounced. The subtitle, "Sunday in the Park," indicates its subject: a series of episodic shots, composed like a montage drawing, of a day of life in a Paterson park. This is "the narrative thread" which runs through the three sections of the book. The role of Paterson-as-man-and-observer, delineated in Book One, is further personalized in Book Two to include Paterson-as-poet-and-actor. Dr. Williams is trying to merge the contemporary physical being of a city (Paterson) and relevant bits of its history with his own personal existence and history as a poet. In the lineaments of this conception we find the micro-macrocosmic myth basic to the functioning of a master work. This is not to say that *Paterson* is a master work, but to indicate that the prescription for one is inherent in it.

What Dr. Williams is saying about himself, he is also saying by implication about all of us. Writing for poets and critics, he is showing presumably why he cannot write for everyone else, though he tries to write *about* the others. The reason is principally a matter of divorce between knowledge and feeling. It concerns the technical difficulty of escaping from the staleness of old forms, old language, old styles. And it concerns the moral impossibility of putting into words, however beautiful and accurate, anything that finally does not underestimate, pervert or elude the reality of what is physically and essentially ever-new, ever-recreated about us. Dedicated to the word, the verbal invention, the poetic expression, the poet is divorced from the concretions which he means to express. Thus he becomes devitalized, incapable of satisfying human relationships, and is cast off by the culture in which he is born. Not only the poet, but the culture itself is divided by the same great divorce. The people of Paterson have been codified, because distrusted and feared ("a great beast," said Hamilton), in terms of economic potentials by the legislators, the industrialists, the

Reprinted, with changes by the author, from *Poetry*, LXXIV (April 1949), 37–41, copyright 1949 by The Modern Poetry Association. Reprinted with the permission of the Editor of *Poetry* and Edwin Honig.

textbook writers of history, the statisticians, the law-enforcers. Thus the poet identifies himself with the poor, those most palpably exploited by the mythical divorce: those who, lacking words, create beauty, for whom pleasure is a drunken love, an aborted dance, an ecstatic but neglected confession, a lazy Sunday afternoon sleep in the park. By this vicarious identification, the poet is "accepted" among the rejected: he finds his place as artist and human being with those who have never found their place as human beings.

The poetry in Book Two is overshadowed by long prose excerpts from a letter which seems actually to have been written to the poet (thinly anonymized as "Dr. P.") by a woman writer with whom he has broken relations. Agonizedly personal, self-conscious, and painfully recriminative, the document seems to throttle the poet and the poetry both, as well as to serve as "a replica" of the divorce theme in its most ambivalent sense. The use of documentary material taken bodily from various unnamed texts to provide historical analogues to the poem (a kind of selective system of footnoting loosely fitted into the poetry) is a practice continued here from Book One. But whereas one inclines to accept their relationship to the poetry (and to recognize in the invented and poeticized "document" of the revivalist preacher in Book Two a further organic connection) one finds oneself after a second or third reading gliding over the prose and concentrating on the poetry. In all cases, that is, but in the case of the rejected woman poet's letter. Dominated and drawn by its prominence in the book, the reader returns to it again and again till gradually its depressive weight obliterates the poetry itself, even as a refuge from the harrowing complaint of the anonymous woman writer.

Thus it seems that the obtrusive autobiographic turn which *Paterson* takes in Book Two (represented by the letter) begins to disrupt the objective symbolic relationships set up in Book One. Such a weakness points, on the one hand, to the structural limitations of the poem's method, and, on the other, to the theoretical uncertainty of its conception.

It is not that a long poem based, as *Paterson* is, on a Heraclitean view of the world cannot be successfully done. Lucretius did it in *De Rerum Natura*. The point about Dr. Williams' failure to do it thus far is this. He accepts a basically scientific view of the world, a world in flux, always changing into significantly new and identifiable relationships; and he accepts the state of things in such a world, as Lucretius did, without the guidance of a supernatural ideal. But like Lucretius and all the pagans, new and old, he must nevertheless find some ideal island, some place of rest. Lucretius found it in the symbol of Venus the procreator, the repository of all earthly beauty. Williams finds it in beauty, too, but in a more difficult and artistically compromising kind—the beauty of honesty. Through such an ideal the dual identity of the poet is revealed: first as an objective visualizer of undiscovered phenomenal relationships, and then as a romantically displaced, culturally rejected and underprivileged citizen. As such, the poet who remakes the world, as Williams proposes, in the mythical image of a man-city relationship, continually succumbs to the belief that the whole of his myth-made universe is conditioned not by the fortuitous and objective relationships according to which he has molded his aesthetic, but by a personally determined impasse, the mirror of his own dislocations. To enforce the ideal of honesty, the concept of man-as-city is altered to poet-as-city, a role so specialized as to limit seriously the universal relevance of the original identification.

In this sense, honesty becomes a nostalgic talisman, like Stephen Daedelus' ashplant, rather than the kingly scepter which one recognizes, without having to have it pointed out, because it is more the symbol of active power than of ornamental disuse. Instead of signifying truthful detachment, the acceptance of things as they are believed to be, honesty becomes a license for the poet's anarchic resentment of things as they are and a valve for emitting steam concerning things as they should be, or used to be.

One may not feel that a consistent philosophic view is necessary in order to write a long, serious poem. But if it is clear, as I believe it is in Williams, that the poet implies his acceptance of a definite philosophic point of view, in his short poems as well as in *Paterson*, then his failure to be consistent in it is related to a deficiency in the poetry itself.

In a passage of self-commiseration toward the end of Book Two, Williams points to the inadequacy of the whole mythic concept upon which *Paterson* is built. He is speaking of "Faitoute" or "Paterson" or "Dr. P"—himself, the poet:

> that the poet,
> in disgrace, should borrow from erudition (to
> unslave the mind) : railing at the vocabulary
> (borrowing from those he hates, to his own
> disenfranchisement)
> —discounting his failures
> seeks to induce his bones to rise into a scene,

his dry bones, above the scene, (they will not)
illuminating it within itself, out of itself
to form the colors, in the terms of some
back street, so that the history may escape
the panders
                    accomplish the inevitable
poor, the invisible, thrashing, breeding
            debased city

. . . .

There are always at least two poets in William Carlos Williams: the lounging, dispassionate re-creator of the everyday world of the senses, the exquisite miniaturist, and the besieged expositor of poetic values, striking out at a devaluating world. In him we observe the impasse created by the conception of the artist as both "fabulous artificer" and declassed human being "trying to communicate" with other human beings in a world constantly goaded to conflict between dehumanized categories. It is a situation sufficiently dramatized in all of Dr. Williams' work—and to a supreme degree in *Paterson*—to constitute a major achievement in contemporary literature. But one wonders, because one still hopes for something more and greater, whether the master work of our age should not derive from a sensibility historically enfranchised from that typical impasse, and thus capable of writing in the highest artistic terms not only about but *for* all the mythically divorced citizens in a world of Patersons.

Hayden Carruth

Dr. Williams's *Paterson*

This third book in Dr. Williams's projected long poem (the fourth and final book is promised "by 1951") is at first reading the most difficult of the three we now have, and at the eighth reading some

Reprinted from *The Nation*, CLXX (April 8, 1950), 331–33, by permission of *The Nation* and Hayden Carruth.

details of structure and aspects of symbol remain unclear. Nevertheless, we can begin to perceive what will be the shape, scope, and texture of the finished work; this book helps greatly to expand and clarify a number of themes, heretofore obscure, in the first two books. When the three are read together in sequence, they reveal, through an interlacing of symbols and a thematic reference back and forth, a close and compact development. More than ever, it becomes apparent that Dr. Williams has in mind a whole, inseverable poem, not a discrete tetralogy, as many of those who reviewed the first two books were led to assume.

The meaning of the poem so far can best be elucidated by a compressed, doubtless defacing examination of its symbols. Paterson, then, is a city and also a man, a giant who lies asleep, whose dreams are the people of the city, whose history is roughly coterminous with, and equal to, the history of America. He is diseased with slums and factories and the spiritlessness of industrial society; his character—usually as observer—walks about, sometimes as a plain citizen, sometimes as a hero, often as "Dr. Paterson"—the poet himself. Beside Paterson lies a mountain, which is a woman, upon whose body grow trees and flowers, with the city park at her head. The city-man and mountain-woman are the two basic facts of the poem; they are activated by the four elements. A river, broken by a falls, flows between them, and has, beyond its obvious sexual meaning, the further significances of flowing time and of language, the fundamental or pre-mental language of nature. Earth is the speaker that knows this language, the "chatterer." Fire is the creative act, in love or art. Wind is, if my reading is correct, inspiration, the integrator, the carrier of sounds and smells. Though generally benign, these forces may be malevolent too, for fire, flood, cyclone, and earthquake all occur in this poem.

Another dichotomy of ideas, which is enforced upon these basic symbols, is that of marriage-divorce. As divorce is a principal symptom of social disorder, so it is also of historical disorder: man has been divorced from his beginnings, his sources. Dr. Williams also uses the word *blockage:* man has been blocked from an understanding of his real self in nature by the modern institutions of church, university, commerce, et cetera. Dr. Williams seems to be saying that the only way to escape these blocks is to ignore them, to sidestep them and experience marriage directly. Thus, in the river, it is the falls which is important, the present act and present moment which unite immediately the man and the woman, the city and the mountain, the "plunge" which "roars" now with a language that lies hidden in the past above and the future below.

This third book has been described by Dr. Williams as a search for a language. Yet much of it is spent in inveighing against what we ordinarily call language. The technical abstractions of scholarship are the poet's primary anathema, but he extends his disgust to include almost all human speech. "No ideas but in things," he says repeatedly—the Objectivist doctrine carried to its extreme. Abstract "meaning" is the enemy, "an offense to love, the mind's worm eating out the core." The dead authors in the library are "men in hell, their reign over the living ended," their thoughts trapped in a hull of inflexible, dead rhetoric. Even the poet's own work is suspect; at one point, he admonishes himself: "Give up the poem. Give up the shilly-shally of art."

This would seem to put the poet in a rather difficult spot, since there honestly isn't much reason to be writing a poem (much less to publish it) if one must write in a bad language. Dr. Williams's conclusions on this head are not so clear as one would wish, but he appears to be saying that the poet can resolve his difficulty through a doctrine of invention. The good language is the language of the river, articulated by the falls. The poet cannot hope to imitate the falls, but he can learn from it. By forgetting the past, by writing instantaneously, even carelessly, by grounding all speech firmly in natural objects, the poet can create a language in nature which is essentially an act, not a meaning—an act of love and union. By working constantly at a peak of inventiveness, he can elevate this language to a level of independence which is its own justification.

"Paterson," when it is finished, will make a great hunting ground for the explicators. There are virtually hundreds of symbols and allusions to be tracked down, related, explained—all of which will, if he sticks to his text, annoy Dr. Williams profoundly. Essays will be written, for instance, on the many uncomplimentary allusions, often devilishly hidden, to T. S. Eliot and his works. There will likewise be essays on the other writers mentioned (I detect Pound, Stevens, and perhaps others), on the various flowers, on the dog. Yet I should like to suggest one question to the explicators before they begin.

Perhaps I can put it best this way. Twenty-five years ago Eliot felt that he should explain some of the symbols and meanings of "The Waste Land" in accompanying notes; for Dr. Williams this is not necessary. We are better readers now. Furthermore, Dr. Williams's symbols are made from objects we all know, and the meanings assigned to them are drawn from a common fund of romantic ideas. But I think we should call on Dr. Williams for another kind of note—a definite note on prosody. He himself sees the trouble, and at one point he says to the reader, rather sharply: "Use a metronome if your ear is deficient, one made in Hungary if you prefer." I think he misses the mark, for any reader with an ear for poetry will easily discern Dr. Williams's astonishingly pure feeling for the rhythms of the American language. It is not meter that bothers me, but the line. These lines are not run over, in the Elizabethan sense; nor are they rove over, in the Hopkinsian sense; they are hung over, like a Dali watch. They break in the most extraordinary places, with no textual, metrical, or syntactical tension to help us over. If this is done for typographical effect, as it sometimes appears, it is inexcusable, for it interferes with our reading. If it is done to indicate a certain way of reading the poem, then we should be told what it is.

Dr. Williams has explained in the past that he uses this device of the short, oddly broken line to obtain the effect of speed in a lyric poem. But "Paterson," by a rough estimate, will be 5,000 lines long when it is finished. In such a large dose, the effect is, instead, limpidity, constantly bolstered by interjections and typographical waggeries; real power is seldom obtained.

Perhaps I am a dull reader; if so, these matters can be explained. And in fairness to me, they must be explained—if not by Dr. Williams, then by some modern prosodist sympathetic to Dr. Williams's method. The question of "Paterson's" value as poetry should at last put the critics face to face with the problems they have been dodging for twenty years: What kinds of lines and sentences does one put next to each other to create a long poem? Is it an arguable prosodic concept that the metrical beat, to the exclusion of the line, is the basic unit of poetry? What, precisely, has experimental technique added to our knowledge of ways to say our thoughts?

Richard Eberhart

A Vision of Life and Man
That Drives the Poet On

The Rutherford, N.J. physician, William Carlos Williams, who also happens to be a poet, novelist, and short-story writer, observes this week his seventy-fifth birthday. He received the National Book Award in 1950 for his "Selected Poems" and "Paterson. Book Three," and it is the long work, "Paterson," the four books of which appeared between 1945 and 1951, for which he is best known. This poem, named for the industrial and in many ways typically American city near Dr. Williams' own home town, illustrates the poet's determination "to write particularly, as a physician works upon a patient, upon the thing before him, in the particular to discover the universal." Now a new book has been added to "Paterson."

The most startling thing about "Paterson (Book Five)" is the compulsion of the author to write it. It is a masterful part of a masterful long poem. Readers enjoyed the first four books as a completed work. They made sense as an esthetic whole and they continue to excite students with their rich sparkle of ideas. The theme was the mind and history of modern man. "Paterson" is one of the major long poems of the century, defining new territory of the American poetic imagination.

Now Dr. Williams has felt compelled to go on with the Paterson story as a living continuum of man and city, civilization and culture. The last part of Book Four was "The Run to the Sea." There was a rightness of ending the poem on an image of going back to the sea, but even then, at the very end, the poet wrote "The sea is not our home" and contrived man and dog coming out of the water. He "headed inland, followed by the dog."

Book Five is written in the same style, with prose letters and historical commentaries interspersed with the lithe and flying poetry. It is as if Dr. Williams could never rest from an endless attempt to put the whole of his vision of life onto paper. Startled to have the addition of Book Five, as if Virgil or Dante had added onto their poems in an astounding passion of illogic, we should en-

Reprinted from *The New York Times Book Review*, September 14, 1958, © 1958 by The New York Times Company. Reprinted by permission.

visage further books because this part does not necessarily conclude the subject or matter.

I would welcome further books because they would be as natural to Dr. Williams restless, inventive mind as is this addition. He could search out further meanings, as he has done here, maintaining the apt quality of the confections in quick esthetic shifts and stances.

Since there is a touch of the comic in the fact of Book Five, a denial of the work of art as inevitable, an insistence on its flowing, protean, ever-changing nature, Dr. Williams should continue with this breath-like work. A tragedy has an end, but history does not. This is an historical poem, and there is no good reason why it should not flow on as long as Dr. Williams can make it do so. The last word is never said in art. "What but indirection/will get to the end of the sphere?" He also writes: "I cannot tell it all" and "it is the imagination/which cannot be fathomed."

There is fresh writing here, with the Unicorn and the Virgin as symbols, with Sappho paired with Satyrs. There is good talk about painting and music, and about the nature of poetry. For instance, in a question-and-answer passage about a Cummings poem we have this:

> "Q.   Well—is it poetry?
> "A.   We poets have to talk in a language which is not English. It is the American idiom . . . It has as much originality as jazz. If you say '2 partridges, 2 mallard ducks, a Dungenese crab'—if you treat that rhythmically, ignoring the practical sense, it forms a jagged pattern. It is, to my mind, poetry.
> "Q.   But if you don't 'ignore the practical sense' . . . you agree that it is a fashionable grocery list?
> "A.   Yes. Anything is good material for poetry. Anything. I've said it time and time again."

As Williams says in a prose passage, "I mean to say Paterson is not a mask like Milton going down to Hell, it's a flower to the mind, etc., etc." And Book Five ends beautifully in an existential-esthetic passage as follows: "We know nothing and can know nothing but/the dance, to dance to a measure contrapuntally, Satyrically, the tragic foot."

2. Essays

Ralph Nash

The Use of Prose in "Paterson"

The real subject here is that prose to which Williams calls attention by differentiating type. *Paterson* does contain obvious prose that is undifferentiated from the surrounding verse: the sermon of Klaus Ehrens, the conversation with old Henry (157), the fragmentary talk of Corydon and Phyllis, the letters from Pound, an old man's reminiscences of early Paterson (230–231). But most of the direct prose is acknowledged with italics or small type, is kept in its place, apart from the main flow of the poetry. This method is something of an innovation in technique; no major, or even relatively successful, poem has previously explored its possibilities. So the kinds of prose in *Paterson*, and their effects, have a general interest in relation to the developments of poetic technique as well as the specific interest of their contributions to the success of the single poem. This sketch will try to abstract from the poem some classification of the types of prose used and to suggest some of the effects that must be reckoned with.

Three major classes of prose can be fairly well separated. There are newspaper clippings and factual data, directly transcribed; there are Williams' own summaries of historical data, excerpted from old newspapers, local histories, etc.; and there are the personal letters. These are the types (not always easily distinguished) that recur most often. If profitable, classification and subdivision could be carried further. For example, there seem to be some transcriptions from the doctor's notebooks (44, 78, 221), and here and there a passage that sounds more like the record of a conversation than like a written letter (122, 171–2). And for exact subdivision there are many problems. Most of the letters are surely authentic, but Phyllis' are surely fictional, and the letter about Musty (69) I suspect is the poet's artifact. The account of Sam Patch's career (25–27) evidently combines authorial summary with direct transcription of an eyewitness account; and the survey of Hamilton's plans for a National Manufactory (84–91) may be direct transcription or summary or both, while the counterpoint indictment of Federal Reserve Banks might be from Williams himself, or from

---

Reprinted from *Perspective*, VI (1953), 191–99, by permission of *Perspective*.

Pound or some other source. But these questions of fact remain minor. Most of the prose involves the use of personal letters, direct transcription of material from newspapers and books (usually local history), or authorial summary of such material.

This classification by source can be supplemented with a temporal classification that may seem to affect more directly the function of the prose within the poem. That is, the prose of Contemporary Fact and the prose of Historical Fact. Both classes, contemporary and historical, are examples of "invention" in the classical sense—the discovery of material appropriate to the meaning and the decorum of the poem.

The letters, which make up most of the prose of contemporary fact, supply corroborations of the poet's insight into contemporary obsessions and confusions. Williams receives a letter that speaks of a "kind of blockage, exiling one's self from one's self" (59), of an inability to communicate (80), of scorn for the divorce that would "bring to literature and to life two different inconsistent sets of values, as you do" (106). This echoing of the themes of divorce and blockage and failure at communication—a large part of the intellectual content of Books One and Two—is a remarkable corroboration of Williams' exploration of his age. It is much more remarkable than the verbal coincidence in an image of "the rough ice of that congealment which my creative faculties began to suffer" (109; see 27, 31, 48, 100). And it is actually more relevant to the poem than are the complaints about clothes, irons, typewriters and stolen money orders (108–112), which anticipate Williams' own complaint on p. 137: "The writing is nothing, the being / in a position to write (that's / where they get you)."

Another significant letter, possibly fictional, is the one about Musty (69). The comic picture of the housewife peeking between her laundered sheets and trying to beat off the male with a stick is also a serious commentary on the civilization's fear of fertility and its attempts to govern and control brute nature. The penitent letter, confessing that Musty has become pregnant in spite of the housewife's precautions, takes its place with many thematic references to the dog, an animal that links the urban and the pastoral world (11, 39, 69, 77, 97–8, 119—wolf, 152, 157–9, 236–8, *et al.*). It is a kind of link between the Dog-as-Opponent (NO DOGS ALLOWED AT LARGE IN THIS PARK; "guilty lovers and stray dogs"—98) and the Dog-as-Companion (the Collie bitch, combed out with deliberate design as Williams must comb out the language —173; old Henry's feist, which the doctor caused to be killed—

159; the favorite dog buried with Pogatticut—158; the black bitch who follows her master inland at the close of the poem).

The letter about Musty's "marriage" not only comments on major themes (fear of fertility, divorce, uneasiness about animals disobedient to The Law), but also it points up Williams' process in "inventing" his poem. For although the various references to dogs depend upon one another for cumulative meaning and importance, they come from diverse sources. Walking in the park, the doctor sees a man combing his Collie, hears somebody calling "Yeah, Chi-Chi," and reflects wryly on the significance of the prohibition against unleashed dogs. Later, reading about local Indian funeral customs (the dancing of the Kinte Kaye—125; the burial of Pogatticut—158), he is interrupted by Henry (126, 157), whose favorite dog he had reported for biting him. Still later, again in the library, as he imagines the scene of the great flood and pictures a dead dog floating in it "toward Acheron" (159), he remembers both the Indian funeral and Henry's bitter accusation, realizing that he himself has had to be one of the upholders of the white man's law and order, causing the death of Henry's dog, for all his sympathy with unleashed dogs. With his intense drive toward honesty, he is accusing himself of sharing the "guilt" of the ordered society in which he bears responsibility as medicine man. Against this (partial) background is thrown the blatantly sterile and stinted attitude of the housewife, whose attempt to prevent an intrusion of Nature into her backyard, however comic it may seem, is nevertheless only another facet of the general divorce of urban man from his sources, a divorce which Williams has accused himself of making between his life and art (111). Thus, whether authentic or an artifact, the letter corroborates a view of himself and of contemporary man, at the same time that it helps to make more meaningful one of the poet's letters (*i.e.*, the passage on 111) and one of his readings in local history.

These two examples will serve to suggest how the letters partially function in the same way as the images, details, phrases and quotations of the poetry itself, in building up patterns of recurring motifs in a poem that shares the contemporary predilection for thematic structure. The letters also share in the special functions of the other prose. For one thing, I have classed them as Prose of Contemporary Fact. I mean this to stress their nature as blocks of material coming into the poem from outside. These letters (at least most of them) are not constructs of the poet; they are given quantities, entities in their own right, that must be fitted into the structure of the poem. One cannot speak as if Williams were a scientist, shaping his theory to fit all the facts: he necessarily keeps at least the negative power of choice and omission. But a letter (or anything else) written by someone other than the poet brings into the poem something of an air of documentation. Irrelevancies and private allusions emphasize that this is not exactly a piece of the poem, but a piece of the poet's world, an upthrust of his autobiography, an outcropping of the substratum on which his City is based. The direct presentation of these fragments, without their being shaped into the rhythms and diction of the surrounding poetry, is of course an artistic device. No doubt Williams intends it partly as a forceful marriage of his poem's world with that world of reality from which he is fearful of divorcing himself. But it has also a special effect of presenting the Poet as Recorder, relatively detached and objective, reading his morning mail as he might read a history of Paterson, acting somewhat as the scientist might in checking his guesses against the facts. Perhaps the best corroboration of this is that Williams keeps up the device of the interpolated letter, even though he has to create the letters, in the specifically dramatic objectification that makes up the pastoral of Phyllis and Corydon.

One other effect is largely, though not exclusively, a property of the personal letters. They document, very directly, the basic problem of the need for a language ("Haven't you forgot your virgin purpose, the language?"—219). An obvious example is the letter of DJB ("Tell Raymond I said I bubetut hatche isus cashutute Just a new way of talking kid"—150), but also the dead triteness of the letter about Musty and the pathetic braveries of Phyllis' slang are examples of the same kind of failure with the language. Even clearer and more damaging are the "literary" letters, those from T. and/or T.J. (37–8, 40), from *La votre C.* (105–113, *et al.*), and from A.P. (204–6). These people sound interesting but their stylistic posturing is incredible: "In spite of the grey secrecy of time and my own self-shuttering doubts in these youthful rainy days, I would like to make my presence in Paterson known to you. . . . Not only do I inscribe this missive somewhat in the style of those courteous sages of yore who recognized one another across the generations as brotherly children of the muses . . ." (204). However much Williams was concentrating on the contents of these letters, he could hardly be oblivious of their relevance to his underlying concern for "the language . . . the language!"

This latter aspect of the prose of contemporary fact also ap-

pears in the extracts from Historical Fact. The clearest example is
the nineteenth-century rhetoric of the account of Mrs. Cumming's
death: "She had been married about two months, and was blessed
with a flattering prospect of no common share of Temporal felicity
and usefulness in the sphere which Providence had assigned her;
but oh, how uncertain is the continuance of every earthly joy"
(23). Williams' comments are explicit:

> A false language. A true. A false language pouring—a language
> (misunderstood) pouring (misinterpreted) without dignity, with-
> out minister, crashing upon a stone ear. At least it settled it for
> her (24; cf. 102–3).

Other passages of nineteenth-century prose reinforce this one, but
need no special comment (18–19, 48, 60–61, 64, *et al.*). However,
it is irresistible to note the wry humor (and the constant alertness
to the problem of language) in Williams' excerpt from an account
of Indian ritual, immediately following a bitter passage on the
artist's struggle to live and his audience's complete refusal of any
struggle to comprehend ("Geeze, Doc, I guess it's all right/ but
what the hell does it mean?"—138). The passage on Indian ritual
concludes:

> While some are silent during the sacrifice, certain make a ridicu-
> lous speech, while others imitate the cock, the squirrel, and other
> animals, and make all kinds of noises. During the shouting two
> roast deer are distributed.

The two roast deer mark this as the "invention" of a genius, a
genius, moreover, with the high good humor of despair.

Like the letters, the prose of historical fact emphasizes the Poet
as Recorder, partly through the same device of inserting unshaped
blocks of foreign material, but in this case also through Williams'
appearance as impersonal summarizer. The quality of this summary prose is sometimes exceptionally fine, as in Williams' account
of early life in the Ramapos (21–22); in almost all instances it
provides a special effect of calm and interested but detached observation. Further comment on this quality of impersonal detachment would have to involve fuller discussion of the prose rhythms,
but the lack of comment here is not meant to minimize its importance. It is one of the most striking and consistent effects of the
prose in *Paterson*.

Also, the various excerpts and summaries from past history are interwoven with general themes of the poem, but for brevity this function may be passed over, since it is not different in kind from that illustrated above for the personal letters.

While we are still concerned with the relation of the prose to *Paterson's* content and structure, we may observe two rather special types. One of these is the prose passage that is simply a kind of footnote, existing as an appendage to one particular passage without much relevance to other parts of the poem. An example is the fragment from Columbus' account of his discovery of the New World (209), which is relevant directly to Marie Curie's discovery of the new world of atomic physics—although perhaps it is also a bit of ironic counterpoint to the atom bomb (78, 201). The neatest example, though, is the case history of prevention of contagious diarrhea in the pediatric ward (208). This is a quiet joke, the clue to which is the last sentence: "The nurse was at once removed from duty with full pay, a measure found to be of advantage in having hospital personnel report diarrheal disturbances without fear of economic reprisal." Since Williams has just quoted Chaucer's "Thy drasty rymyng is not worth a toord," it is clear that reporting diarrheal disturbances without fear of economic reprisal is another version of the plight of the poet (137–8). An amusing footnote, but nothing more. There are only a few of these sharply limited addenda.

The other special type is the prose passage which has supplied a theme for the poem. Clearly it is of some interest to note when Williams' reading of local history has supplied him, not with additional illustration, but with a theme to be illustrated. One of the most probable examples of this (apart from the Annus Mirabilis of 1902) is Peter the Dwarf (18–19, 225), whose deformed body could not support the enormous weight of his head (J. W. Barber and H. Howe, *Historical Collections of the State of New Jersey*, New York 1844, p. 407). The dwarf becomes for Williams a sardonic symbol of himself as poet (101–103), "hideously deformed," a kind of toad "saved by his protective coloring," threatened with decomposition into leaves and toadstools unless he comes to terms ("Go home. Write. Compose... Ha! Be reconciled, poet, with your world"). With this image of the dwarf-poet in his mind, coupled with the associated image of the poet as lame dog (11), Williams would obviously appropriate with grim delight Symonds' declaration that "The choliambi are in poetry what the dwarf or cripple is in human nature" (53). Perhaps less obviously, he might have had his deformed monster in mind when he noted, as another symbol for the poet, the heavy crow and the smaller birds stabbing for his eyes (61; cf. 223).

Thus far I have been concerned largely with the relation of the prose to thematic content and structure, with some emphasis on the interplay of past and present in the total poem. For the difficult subject of the relations of the prose passages to the poetic technique of *Paterson*, I can only offer a few suggestions. It is evident that the prose affects the poem most strongly by its sound, by the inevitable interruption to eye and ear whenever one of the prose passages appears. This means, for one thing, that the prose is of tremendous importance to the pace and tempo of the entire poem. Nowhere is this more striking than in the eight pages of closely set type that provide a tortured, involved, garrulous, intimate, but ultimately dignified and quiet close for Book Two: *"please* [read this], merely out of fairness to me—much time and much thought and much unhappiness having gone into those pages." Such a huge chunk of extraneous prose obviously will bring the reader to a full halt: but this is exactly right at the close of a book, especially this one which marks a kind of midpoint in the poem. But inextricably connected with this effect is the fact that the long letter from C., portions of which have appeared before, has been serving as ironic counterpoint to the conversation of He and She ("I wish to be with you abed, we two / as if the bed were the bed of a stream"— 35). And if it were not for the extract from C's unhappy letter (an extract which begins "My attitude toward woman's wretched position in society . . ."), Book Two would close with a lyric promise of the consummation of love—"On this most voluptuous night of the year." So the problem of pace and rhythm here is closely connected with the content of C's letter, with its previous structural use, with its own prose style, and with its own particular placing in the poem. No doubt similar difficulties would surround many passages if one were to pursue the question of pace further.

The range of subject matter and rhythmic movement in the prose passages makes a kind of parallel to the range of the poetry. The prose is sometimes, one might say, "the waste farina in the sink." Yet again, as in the burial of Pogatticut, for example, it may be very close to the precisions and rhythms of the poetry. A long analysis, with many examples of rhythms, images, and details, might do something toward making explicit the degrees of prosiness, as it were. And this might in turn illuminate a part of Williams' general method in poetry, since the use of prose in *Paterson* is from one point of view only a kind of logical extension of that drive toward the direct, unadorned fact, the single stubborn *thing*, that has always been known to be part of Williams' faith. That is, how much does the prose work with the poetry, and how much against it? Do the rhythms of the prose set up defiantly a world of "fact" against which the poetry batters? For all that may be said of their contribution to the total poem, do the prose passages by their nature keep up a posture of opposition to the poetry, because of their movement and sound, and subject matter too? And if the prose does this, in varying degrees, may it not provide some measure for the same kind of thing—gradated, no doubt—*within* Williams' verse? (*i.e.*, can we at least admit that the prose is not poetry, and starting from there build up some kind of meaning and definition for the quality in Williams' verse that Wallace Stevens blandly and reasonably chose to call "anti-poetic"?) In this way, the prose in *Paterson* strikes one as quite an important subject for anyone interested in Williams' general aesthetics.

Other facets of the prose as vehicle of the language have been alluded to above—the "scientific" tone of detachment, the ironic illustration of failure in communication. The last function to be noted here is a mixture of various things—prose style, subject matter, authorial attitude, sources—but it is at any rate a very important contribution to the effect of the poem. This is the function of the prose in constantly reinforcing an immediate sense of locale. Newspaper clippings, letters addressed to Paterson, excerpts from local history: all insist upon Paterson as place. Paterson the Man is no Ulysses; the sea is not his home. However much the techniques (and economics) of *Paterson* remind us of the *Cantos*, Williams is not writing of the Wanderer who knew many manners of men and saw many cities. And he is not constructing a City of the Just. It is Paterson, not Dioce. The prose passages are by no means a minor device for keeping us clear on that essential point.

To sum up. The use of prose in *Paterson* contributes to a sense of immediacy (the use of personal letters, contemporary newspapers) while at the same time it gives a sense of distance and objectivity (the use of historical materials, the relatively dispassionate recording of personal involvements). The appearance of passages, both contemporary and historical, that in themselves document such a theme as the search for a language, accentuates in a completely valid way the continuity of that problem; and in general the appearance of both contemporary and historical "documentation" of the thematic concerns of the poem tends to give it continuity, to increase the sense of structural and contentual unity and validity. In addition, the prose passages sometimes represent ultimate sources, the origins of some of the thematic material.

As for the contribution of the prose to the techniques of presentation, the actual speaking of the poem, the inevitable key word is counterpoint. There is the counterpoint affecting pace and tempo —the intrusion of flat prose rhythms, in passages of varying length, the occasional rhythmic and vivid prose, the ironic juxtaposition of lyric affirmations and unpleasant "facts," or the opposite juxtaposition of a grimly urban scene and an excerpt from the days of a more pastoral village life. Closely related is the counterpoint of the materials of the poem: the balancing of the pure with the dirty, the resolution with the confusion, the dream with the fact, the past with the present (but cutting both ways, not neglecting the old newspapers, the murders, the suicides, the child aflame in a field trying to crawl home). And over all this—and over the tone of impersonal observation, the outright *examples* of the failure of language, and the many effects I have probably missed—is what we might call the counterpoint of poet and city. Yesterday's weather, last week's meeting, a nineteenth-century artesian well: they crop up out of past and present like the flint ("the flinty pinnacles") out of the ground, insisting on the here and now and then of Paterson as place.

This has been more a description than a judgment. We probably all need to know the poem better before anyone come to judgment. But some major points rise naturally out of the description. I have had to speak of Williams' "invention" as being invention in the classical sense of "coming upon" the appropriate material: and I suppose it is clear that I think his powers of invention are splendid. However, the obvious thing, after granting the poet the right to "invent" his material wherever he can, is to say that he "must transform it," must shape it with the shaping power of imagination. The classical line is that it is not rhyming and versing that maketh the poet, but his power of Fiction, or of Making; and the demand for powers of "fiction" continues strongly in our time ("A fictive covering Weaves always glistening from the heart and mind"). But surely Williams does exercise his invention without going on to fictive transformation of the invented material. That is a part of the method of *Paterson*, a part of its technical innovation. Is *Paterson* a better, or worse, poem for this partial denial of the great requirement of Fiction? No doubt the question can be avoided, with our highly developed sense for the fineness of the line between sanity-or-insanity, mental-or-physical, fact-or-fiction.

But avoiding it is not to my purpose, because a major point in what has been said here is that the denial of Fiction—the widespread use of unaltered "factual" prose—is a positive, novel contribution to the meaning and the technique of Williams' long poem.

Roger Seamon

The Bottle in the Fire: Resistance as Creation in William Carlos Williams' *Paterson*

There is almost unanimous, though vague, agreement that William Carlos Williams's *Paterson* is about the poetic process. The many ideas about poetry in *Paterson* have led one critic to describe the poem as "an 'Ars Poetica' for contemporary America." [1] Williams's concern with the techniques of modern verse, his place in the tradition of Whitman, and his use as a model by many avante-garde poets have tended to place great emphasis on his prosodic methods and consequently left his thematic use of the poetic process aside. Poetry, for Williams, was an act as well as a product, and in *Paterson* he explores the nature of the act through his images. These images of the poetic process culminate in a metaphor for the product, the bottle in the fire, and to understand that metaphor it is necessary to trace the processes which contributed to its creation.

Writing of *Paterson* in a letter Williams asserted, "If I did not achieve a language I at least stated what I would not say." [2] The idea of resistance is found in *Paterson* from beginning to end. In

Reprinted from *Twentieth Century Literature,* XI (1965), 16–24, by permission of *Twentieth Century Literature* and Roger Seamon.
[1] Dudley Fitts, (Review of *Paterson IV*) *Saturday Review of Literature,* XXXIV (1951), 23.
[2] *The Selected Letters of William Carlos Williams,* ed. John C. Thirwall (New York, 1957), p. 304.

the opening stanza Williams sees himself as a dog who has refused
to escape:

> Sniffing the trees,
> just another dog
> among a lot of dogs. What
> else is there? And to do?
> The rest have run out—
> after the rabbits.[3]

He refuses the temptation to leave an environment which is resistant to poetry, "this / swill-hole of corrupt cities" (III, i, 132), and
there seeks

> The radiant gist that
> resists the final crystallization.
>   (III, i, 133)

Even in the final passage of *Paterson* these temptations are still
heard. The sea (the womb, Europe, classical culture, traditional
forms of beauty) calls to him:

>   Listen!
> Thalassa! Thalassa!
>   Drink of it, be drunk!
>   Thalassa
> immaculata: our home, our nostalgic
> mother in whom the dead, enwombed
>   again
> cry out to us to return   .
>   the blood dark sea!
> nicked by the light alone, diamonded
> by the light   .   from which the sun
> alone lifts undamped his wings
>   of fire!
> .   .   not our home! It is NOT
> our home.   (IV, iii, 236)

The idea that refusal can be a form of achievement has been singled
out by Alfred Alvarez as a central characteristic of Williams's
poetry. He sees Williams as a poet who

---

[3] William Carlos Williams, *Paterson*, (New York, 1951), I, i, 11. Page numbers refer to the New Directions edition of Books I through IV. I have included references to Book and section as well.

judge(s) less from what (he) believe(s) in than from what (he is) not taken in by ... Someone has suggested that this is what is left of the Puritan's insistence on individual conscience. Perhaps; but that particularly deep-rooted scepticism seems to me ... much more an individual's instinct for sanity and survival than a principle or tradition. It is something inherited from the faults of society rather than from its strengths. It is this kind of minimal sanity on which the best and least pretentious verse of William Carlos Williams ... is built. As poetry it is not very profound, but it is occasionally impressive as a statement of the American negative virtues.[4]

Although *Paterson* is not Williams's "least pretentious verse," it too is created out of resistance, only now the resistance stems from the materials with which the poet must work. In his role as poet rather than alienated member of society Williams is acting on the side of the "strengths" of his culture, and he must face the refusals for which he has so much sympathy. The world will not easily capitulate to the ordering process of poetry, and so conflict follows. The image that Williams uses for this method of creation and its result is a bottle in a fire:

> Poet Beats Fire at Its own Game! The
> bottle!
> the bottle! the bottle! the bottle! I
> give you the bottle!   (III, ii, 143)

The power to resist, and the ability to transform such resistance into an object is achieved only after active struggle, the struggle between the poet and the things out of which he must make the poem. Both protagonists resist and attack, and the battle may appear to be out of proportion to its conclusion. This may be the reason that Alvarez feels Williams is pretentious. We might however recall what the poet had to say about Book IV in the Author's Note prefixed to *Paterson;* it "will be reminiscent of episodes—all that one man may achieve in a lifetime."

The conflict between the poet and his materials is embodied in a series of polarities that weave in and out of the poem: man-woman (the dominant set), convention-instinct, ideas-things, art-nature, the noble-the commonplace. The latter member of each of these opposing forces constitutes what Williams feels is the basic

---

[4] *The Shaping Spirit* (London, 1958), p. 178.

reality out of which his poem must be constructed, but whose very
nature is to resist being made into poetry, to resist being shaped
by convention, ideas, and art. This antagonism reveals a split in
Williams's loyalties which is clearly stated in a letter he wrote to
Harriet Monroe:

> Now life is above all things else at any moment subversive of life
> as it was the moment before—always new, always irregular. Verse
> to be alive must have infused into it something of the same order,
> some tincture of disestablishment, something in the nature of an
> impalpable revolution, an ethereal reversal . . . I am speaking of
> modern verse.[5]

The prose in *Paterson* is quite palpable testimony to Williams's
desire to retain some of the quality which life has. The world gets
into the poem in great chunks, and very often undermines the attempt of the poet to order and dignify.

The editor of Williams's letters has supplied an unusually appropriate example of the nature and function of the reality which
Williams wishes to retain in the poem. In describing his editorial
procedure he says that, "Deletions . . . are almost entirely those of
inconsequential material, like a paragraph on custody of a cat in
the middle of a serious discussion of tragedy in the modern world." [6]
There is no discussion of tragedy in *Paterson*, only a brief reference
to "old plays," but here is the beginning of a letter which is not
found in the *Selected Letters*, but in the poem itself:

> Dear B.   Please excuse me for not having told you this when I was
> over to your house. I had no courage to answer your questions so
> I'll write it. Your dog *is* going to have puppies although I prayed
> she would be okey.   (II, i, 69)

Williams refuses to "edit"; the paragraph on a dog or cat contains
more reality than a discussion of tragedy. It is closer to a world
which, if finally not important, must at least be recognized and
understood (put into the poem) before the abstractions can have
any meaning. As the editorial procedure indicates it is often con-
venient to ignore this reality in order to bolster the dignity of one's
ideas; but dignity achieved through such strategy is hardly valid,
for it can be undercut by the simplest occurrence. The function of

---

[5] *Selected Letters,* pp. 23–24.
[6] *Ibid.,* pp. xvi–xvii.

the commonplace in *Paterson* is to guarantee that such ennobling
evasions are not permitted to remain uncriticized by the basic
reality they would ignore.

This coupling of the refined and the gross, poetry and reality,
is a basic technique in *Paterson*. When Williams introduces his
mythical female protagonist in Book I he romanticizes her:

> The Park's her head, carved, above the
>   Falls, by the quiet
> river; Colored crystals the secret of those
>   rocks;
> farms and ponds, laurel and the temperate
>   wild cactus,
> yellow flowered   .   .   facing him, his
> arm supporting her, by the *Valley of the
>   Rocks,* asleep.
> Pearls at her ankles, her monstrous hair
> spangled with apple-blossoms is scattered
>   about into
> the back country, waking their dreams—
>   where the deer run
> and the wood-duck nests protecting his
>   gallant plumage.   (I, i, 17)

This is immediately followed by a prose passage describing the discovery of those pearls in 1857. This historical note concludes: "A
large round pearl, weighing 400 grains which would have been the
finest pearl of modern times, was ruined by boiling open the shell."
At this point in the poem the reality and the imaginative construction are simply at odds, and they undermine each other. One
of the most effective uses of this technique is found in a passage
where the poet describes "Two half-grown girls hailing hallowed
Easter,"

> two, bound by an instinct to be the same:
> ribbons, cut from a piece,
> cerise pink, binding their hair: one—
> a willow twig pulled from a low
> leafless bush in full bud in her hand,
>   (or eels or a moon!)
> holds it, the gathered spray,
> upright in the air, the pouring air,
> strokes the soft fur—
>   Ain't they beautiful!   (I, ii, 29)

Williams's "poetry" is poignantly deflated by the words of the girl
which expresses her inner poverty. (That these words may be
spoken by the poet also does not damage the effect.) The poet has
made of the scene something that is untrue to its reality—and it
strikes back. This kind of juxtaposition occurs repeatedly in *Paterson*, and is a central technique in Williams's articulation of the conflict between reality and the poetic process.

Another aspect of reality is instinct, and we can use the passage
about the pregnant dog to demonstrate how this opposing force
functions in *Paterson*. Here we see that the fruition of instinctual
behavior disrupts the conventional expectations of the letter-writer,
and, if her fear is not misguided, of "B" also. The dog engages in
sexual acts with no intention of disturbing her owner or keeper.
By simply following her instincts she arouses great anxiety in her
human environment. The embarrassment which the dog causes is
like the deflation the poet experienced when the girl he described
so lyrically asked, "Ain't they beautiful?" In both cases conventional forms (one aesthetic, the other domestic) are confronted by
a more basic reality and are thereby discomfited and implicity
criticized. These episodes are metaphors for the predicament of
the poet; as an avatar of the conventional his work will suffer the
same fate unless he does justice to the more commonplace and
cruder aspects of experience.

To return to the letter and the girls on Easter Sunday; in both
incidents it is the female who embodies the poet's opposition, and
that is the general pattern of the imagery in *Paterson*. This is
made explicit in Williams's mythological figures, Paterson (the
city, the poet) and the Park. He re-introduces these figures at the
beginning of Book II:

> Outside
>   outside myself
>   there is a world,
> he rumbled, subject to my incursions
> —a world
>   (to me) at rest,
>   which I approach
> concretely—
>   The scene's the Park
>   upon the rock,
>   female to the city
> —upon whose body Paterson instructs his
>   thoughts
> (concretely)   (II, i, 57)

The struggle to create poetry is compared to the battle between men and women, to the frustrations and achievements that are found in sexual and marital life. From this point of view a line from *Paterson* which is often quoted as an axiom of Williams's poetry, "No ideas but in things" (I, i, 14), can be seen as a slightly comic sexual pun. The poet's problem is the problem of marriage, and Williams uses the idea of divorce almost as a refrain:

> Divorce is
> the sign of knowledge in our time,
> divorce! divorce!   (I, ii, 28)

It is the divorce of the polarities mentioned above which leads to sterility, and Williams's concern with this separation recalls Pound's attack on usury in Canto XLV where similar imagery is used:

> Stone cutter is kept from his stone
> weaver is kept from his loom

And the artist divorces himself from the materials of his art.

The fullest exposition of this theme is contained in a series of letters that begins early in the first book of *Paterson*; this is also the earliest use of prose. The woman who writes these letters is the major image of the resistances which the poet must meet and transform if he is to succeed. In these letters we see the opposition to the poet not as casual and inadvertent protest against conventions (as was the case with the dog and the girls), but as an active and highly articulate attack. It is this woman who defines most forcefully the issues at stake, and makes clear the relationship between the

> Innumerable women, each like a flower.
> But only one man—like a city.   (I, i, 15)

She defines the problem by opposing literature and life:

> In regard to the poems I left with you; will you be so kind as to return them to me at my new address? And without bothering to comment upon them if you should find that embarrassing—for it was the human situation and not the literary one that motivated my phone call and visit.
>
> Besides, I know myself to be more the woman than the poet; and to concern myself less with the publishers of poetry than with ... living ...   (I, i, 15)

But her own necessity to write belies this assertion, and her insistence on the opposition of literature and life is self-destructive. By attacking the poet's desire to make poetry out of her she attacks an aspect of herself:

> My attitude toward woman's wretched position in society and my ideas about all the changes necessary there, were interesting to you, weren't they, in so far as they made for *literature?* That my particular emotional orientation, in wrenching myself free from patterned standardized feminine feelings, enabled me to do some passably good work with *poetry*—all that was fine, wasn't it—something for you to sit up and take notice of! And you saw in one of my first letters to you (the one you had wanted to make use of, then, in the Introduction to your Paterson) an indication that my thoughts were to be taken seriously, because that too could be turned by you into literature, as something disconnected from life.
>
> (II, iii, 105–6)

This poetess's prose is the reverse of Williams's tendency to romanticize, and both responses to experience represent a failure of the creative process. This separation between art and life is reiterated again and again in *Paterson*. Another correspondent of the poet writes: "With you the book is one thing, and the man who wrote it another. The conception of time in literature and in chronicles makes it easy for men to make such hoax cleavages" (I, ii, 40). The backdrop of Williams's struggle to unite the polarities is figured in the title of Hugh Kenner's book on T. S. Eliot, *The Invisible Poet*. Somewhere between the poles of depersonalization and confession (the poetess's mode) Williams seeks the balance of poetry.

As the poet lets his antagonists have their say both he and they become more conscious of the dilemma, and grow increasingly aware that the "cleavage" is fatal to both:

> How strange you are, you idiot!
> So you think that because the rose
> is red that you shall have the mastery?
> The rose is green, and will bloom,
> overtopping you, green, livid,
> green when you shall speak no more, or
> taste, or even be. My whole life
> has hung too long upon a partial victory.
>
> (I, iii, 41)

The green is the reality which has been persistently subverting the poetry. The redness of the rose is the deceptive beauty of surface which the world presents, especially the natural world. This leads the poet to generalize and conceive all experience in its aesthetic garb. The idea that the world is a work of art is a metaphor many poets (including Williams's friend Wallace Stevens in the poem "Esthetique du Mal") have used as a means of bridging the gap between reality and the poem. But this is an evasion that is closely related to the depersonalization mentioned above, and Williams rejects it. The last lines of the stanza on the rose suggest that to view the world this way is a form of death. The poet's life hangs on (depends upon and is strangled by) the slight thread that extends from an aesthetic reality to the poet. It is a deadening connection and divorces the poet from the livid (living) green.

The woman's reaction against the poet has a similarly destructive effect on her; she finds herself blocked, unable to write, whereas for Williams it has all been too easy and but a "partial victory":

> Despite my having said that I'd never write to you again, I do so now because I find, with the passing of time, that the outcome of my failure with you has been the complete damming up of all my creative capacities in a particularly disastrous manner such as I have never before experienced. (II, i, 59)

The quiet irony which this passage contains is found throughout the letters from "C," as she signs herself. Beneath her involved and very self-conscious agonies lies a simple biological fact: women are unproductive without men. The abstract (anti-poetic) language masks rather modest truths, and under the sharp analytical tone which reflects the contortions of consciousness runs the current of basic and now desperate human needs. It is a failure of language, for the words and the human situation have been severed from each other. Her language resembles the fake nineteenth century sentimental rhetoric of which Williams says elsewhere, "A false language. A true" (I, i, 24). It is both, for it at once conceals basic meanings while obliquely communicating them.

The imagery which "C" uses demonstrates this more clearly. Her language vindicates the poet's use of various images, for they come "naturally" to her as expressions of her predicament. It is the poet's task to place these images in the conscious context and shape of the poem in order to reveal their full significance. We can watch this process at work in a series of images dealing with crusts, sand, and, finally, the bottle:

> For a great many weeks now (whenever I've tried to write poetry) every thought I've had, even every feeling, has been struck off some surface crust of myself which began gathering when I first sensed that you were ignoring the real contents of my last letters to you, and which finally congealed into some impenetrable substance when you asked me to quit corresponding with you altogether without even an explanation.   (II, i, 59)

The barely disguised sexual connotations make the letter somewhat pathetic. All her hardness, her frigidity as it were, is an attempt to conceal longing, and in a later guise she will cry, "Marry us! Marry us!" (II, iii, 102). But before that can be accomplished the poet must turn these images of sterility into new forms. He must break down and through the crusts in order to free the creative potential of the impulses beneath. The substances which now block will be transformed into the bottle, just as the letters taken out of "life" are transformed and given meaning by their place in the structure of the poem. The connection between the surface crust of "C" and the bottle (the female in a comically traditional symbolic shape) which is a re-figuring of that crust is made evident in another letter where she writes that she "shall never again be able to recapture some faith in the reality of my own thoughts and ideas and problems which were turned into dry sand by your attitude toward those letters..." (II, ii, 94). What can effect the transformation of dry sand to shaped glass is fire, the image of destruction which is the dominant metaphor of Book III of *Paterson.*

Book II concludes with a long letter from "C" which recapitulates her attack. In essence this letter represents the triumph of the female material, the anti-poetic, over the shape of the verse. This defeat rouses the poet just as he has roused her. They will come together not in the muted dependency and distance of letters (the letters are never "answered") but in a violent process which more closely resembles the sexual act. That is the subject of Book III. The letters from "C" are completed, and the poet, having succumbed to her outburst and allowed her to expend her energy in a final attack ("... well, that anger of mine isn't there in the last part...") will unleash the forces which have been dammed up, and which will cleanse his own stagnation. This state is symbolized by

The Library (the title of Book III), for it is the attachment to
books that has blocked him.

The second section of Book III contains the image of the bottle
in the fire. Sections One and Three are devoted to other forces,
wind and water, and all three are identified with the woman:

> —a dark flame,
> a wind, a flood—counter to all staleness.
>   (III, i, 123)

The bottle first appears as a casual detail glimpsed in the blaze
that is roaring through the city: " . . an old bottle/mauled"
(III, ii, 141). As the fire increases in intensity the bottle becomes
transformed:

> . . . A bottle, mauled
> by the flames, belly-bent with laughter:
> yellow, green . . .   (III, ii, 142)

Here the male and female begin to merge, for the fire is both an
image of male lust and a part of the natural world out of which the
poem must be made, however destructive both may be. And the
bottle represents a fusion of the hand of the artist and the substances which had resisted him. The attack and the resistance to
attack have become a means of creation. The bottle is "Rec-
reant,/ . . . Calling the fire good" (III, ii, 142).

> So be it. The beauty of fire-blasted sand
> that was glass, that was a bottle:
>   unbottled.
> Unabashed. So be it.   (III, ii, 142)

The bottle is a metamorphosis of the woman-rock who had earlier,
in the person of "C," been transformed to dry sand by the poet.
Now, through an element in her own nature (which was revealed
in her attack on the poet), she has been made into an object that
is resistant, and that can sustain the attack which had previously
defeated her. The new capacity to resist is not however mere dull
opposition:

> An old bottle, mauled by the fire
> gets a new glaze, the glass warped
> to a new distinction, reclaiming the

                    undefined. A hot stone, reached
                    by the tide, crackled over by fine
                    lines, the glaze unspoiled   .
                    Annihilation ameliorated:
                                        (III, ii, 142–3)

The last line returns us to an awareness of the minimal achievement which the poet seeks. The process defines the limitations of
the product.

The meaning of the bottle image is extended through its connections to another series of images, women as flowers:

                    ... The glass
                    splotched with concentric rainbows
                    of cold fire that the fire has bequeathed
                    there as it cools, its flame
                    defied—the flame that wrapped the glass
                    deflowered, reflowered there by
                    the flame: a second flame, surpassing
                    heat   .   (III, ii, 143)

Poets have traditionally used flowers as images for women, and
Williams, with deliberate innocence, has done the same: "Innumerable women, each like a flower." But a real woman had broken
into the poem (in the letters) to "deflower" herself, to strip away
the conventional image of female beauty, to deny the poet's right
to use her for the purposes of poetry, and to force him to treat her
as a woman and not a literary image. But when this woman became
oppressive she was further "deflowered," at first by her own ad-
mission, and later by the poet as he reduced her to her most basic
elements, wind, fire and water. Out of this second violation came
the flame which turned the dry sand into the bottle. On the new
surface the flame has been "re-flowered," been given a more per-
manent form than it had ever possessed. By "an investment of
grace in the sand" (III, ii, 143) the poem is made. The poet can
shout at the fire that he has beaten it, "Poet Beats Fire at Its Own
Game," and out of his resistance emerges the work of art: "beauty
is/a defiance of authority" (III, ii, 144).

As with other strands of imagery in *Paterson* the bottle in the
fire is picked up for the last time in Book IV and there given a
final twist. Embedded in the resistant object we now find a moral
tag, the anti-poetic "idea" fused with the thing:

```
                  —another, once gave me
           an old ash-tray, a bit of
                       porcelain inscribed
           with the legend, La Vertue
                       est toute dans l'effort
           baked into the material,
                       maroon on white, a glazed
           Venerian scallop  .  for
                       ashes, fit repository
           for legend, a quieting thought:
                              (IV, iii, 221)
```

Here we find the material, the commonplace reality, and the idea literally in the thing; "No ideas but in things." The effort has been to put the poet in the poem, to let the substance have its say, and thereby make the process of creation a central part of the finished product. (Williams's aesthetic seems analogous to the ideas of American "Action Painting." These artists also want the work to record the process of creation, and go even further and make that its essence.) Earlier in *Paterson* Williams had warned himself of this necessity:

```
           But the pathetic library (that contained,
           perhaps, not one volume of distinction)
           must go down also—
                 BECAUSE IT IS SILENT. IT
           IS SILENT BY DEFECT OF VIRTUE
                 IN THAT IT
           CONTAINS NOTHING OF YOU
                              (III, ii, 147–8)
```

By putting himself and his material directly in the poem Williams has hardened it against the revolutionary reality which continually undermines all attempts to formalize it. That is the poem's "*vertue*"—its power to resist the "enormous burning."

To use an ash tray as a metaphor for a poem may seem ignoble, but it defines Williams's attitudes toward poetry and the poetic process. He stated it before:

```
           We read: not the flames
           but the ruin left
           by the conflagration
```

Not the enormous burning
but the dead (the books
remaining). Let us read

and digest: the surface
glistens, only the surface.
Dig in—and you have

a nothing, surrounded by
a surface, an inverted
bell resounding, a

white-hot man become
a book, the emptiness of
a cavern resounding   (III, ii, 149)

The poem is an ordering of the ruin of experience. Bottles, bells, ash trays, dogs, deflowered women—that is Williams's province in *Paterson*, and the struggle to create poetry out of such materials is his central theme. He said this in an essay about Gertrude Stein:

How in a democracy . . . can writing which has to compete with excellence elsewhere and in other times remain in the field and be at once objective (true to fact) intellectually searching, subtle and instinct with powerful additions to our lives? It is impossible without invention of some sort, for the very good reason that observation about us engenders the very opposite of what we seek: triviality, crassness and intellectual bankruptcy. And yet what we do see can in no way be excluded.[7]

And he repeated it in *Paterson:*

Escape from it—but not by running
away. Not by "composition." Embrace
    the
foulness.   (III, i, 126)

Williams's inventiveness is not only prosodic nor as mysterious as some of his remarks on writing poetry would indicate. It is much more traditional. It is the ability to see the relationships between the ruins, the connections between disparate episodes. It is the discovery of the expressiveness, usually muted or obscured, in all

---

[7] *The Selected Essays of William Carlos Williams* (New York, 1954), p. 118.

human acts and artifacts. The techniques I have discussed above reveal how Williams goes about this task of letting the world have its say in the poem. He is sustained in this effort by his faith that the designs left on the bottle (the method and pattern of the poem) are in immediate contact with the world. There is no simple relationship between the two, but the "splotches" and "concentric rainbows" may reveal and preserve the designs of experience, and thereby give "powerful additions to our lives." If the price for this achievement is the rejection of traditional patterns of ordering experience then Williams feels he must pay it, however "negative" the result may be. He had asked himself this question:

> How much does it cost
> to love the locust tree
> in bloom?   (III, i, 117)

Beside the blooming locust lies the "foulness" and if the poem is to endure it must embrace them both. That is the price.

Walter Sutton

Dr. Williams' "Paterson" and the Quest for Form

Maybe there'll be a fifth book of *Paterson* embodying everything I've learned of "the line" to date.—W. C. W. in a letter of March 11, 1952 [1]

The appearance of *Paterson, Book Five*, seven years after Dr. Williams' long-projected poem had been announced as completed, raises a question of form. To what extent is it possible for a reader

Reprinted, with changes by the author, from *Criticism,* II (1960), 242–59, by permission of The Wayne State University Press, copyright 1960, and by Walter Sutton.
[1] *The Selected Letters of William Carlos Williams,* ed. J. C. Thirlwall (New York, 1957), pp. 312–313. Hereafter cited as *SL.*

who has regarded *Paterson* as complete in four parts to revise his conception of the work to allow for the incorporation of Book V, which seems to have evolved as something of an afterthought? In this situation something has to give—either the idea of *Paterson* as a *poem* or the idea of achieved poetic form as a completely-integrated, inviolable whole.

There is, however, no question for the poet as to which idea is dispensable. The appearance of *Paterson Five* indicates a shift and further development in the author's conception of his work, but this shift is entirely consistent with his general viewpoint. The addition of another part or an indefinite number of parts is in accord with Dr. Williams' theory of the poem. For to him the whole of *Paterson*, or of any poem, can be construed as a search for adequate form, a search that is always advancing, as it must advance, in time, but that is never completed. He has described the poem as "an attempt, an experiment, a failing experiment, toward assertion with broken means but an assertion, always, of a new and total culture, the lifting of an environment to expression" (*SL*, 286).

And throughout *Paterson* we see the attempt to raise a changing environment to expression and the sense of failure in the attempt, a failure largely determined by the nature of society. Yet there is a sense of achievement, of a partial victory, in the face of defeat. As Williams has written in the third book of *Paterson*,

> No defeat is made up entirely of defeat—since
> the world it opens is always a place
> formerly
> unsuspected.[2]

So too the poet's language and measure, unsatisfactory though they may be to him in his attempt, open up possibilities of expression hitherto unrealized.

As an artist and man of science, Williams recognizes that man lives in the flux and welter of time, caught in its distractions and fragmentations, and that he must find his identity there. No vision of mystic unity can bring a resolution of multiplicity. Striving for unity or at least a sense of his own identity, the most a man can achieve is *episodes*, or fragments, as Williams comments in his author's note to *Paterson*. Religious mysticism offers no real solution to the twentieth-century intellectual or poet. How can he,

---

[2] *Paterson* (New York, 1951), p. 96. Hereafter cited as *P*.

Williams asks, honestly view either himself or the Church of England as standing outside Einstein's universe? [3] The problem of belief cannot be divorced from the problem of scientific truth. In a relativistic world the only true belief can be found in science, "the realm of the incomplete" (*SE*, 262). In Williams' poetics this view calls for a break from conventional meter (consonant with the world view of an earlier age but not ours) in favor of a "relativistic or variable foot" (*SL*, 335).

This revolutionary break from convention links Williams with the romantics, but distinctions must be made. Although in the romantic tradition in his ideas of poetic diction and his rejection of conventional (he also calls them "neoclassic") metrical patterns, Williams holds aloof from the extreme of the organic theory of form. While he believes that the source of poetry is the spoken language, the dialect—as opposed to the English of the academy—he does not believe that the poet can achieve a completely-integrated or unified form.

Like the romantics, he emphasizes spontaneity and the surrender of the poet to the creative impulse: "Write carelessly so that nothing that is not green will survive" (*P*, 155). He is not, however, of the cult that follows Coleridge in deifying the imagination as the "soul that is everywhere . . . and forms all into one graceful and intelligent whole." He shies, sensibly, hard-headedly, from the holistic extreme of the organic theory. As a poet as well as a physician, Dr. Williams is aware of the incompleteness and lack of self-sufficiency of the individual organism. Form and identity, for the poem as for the human individual, are the result of the interpenetration of subject and object, the poet and his world, the language of the poem and the common language from which it derives.

Poetic form, accordingly, is tentative and relative. It comprises all aspects of the verbal structure achieved by the poet. Among these are diction (the "words" themselves or the "language," in his terms); the metrical arrangement of the words (the "foot," "line," or "measure"); the syntax of the poem (the relation of its verbal units, whether or not grammatical sentences are used); and its overall organization—all involved in the problem of "how to begin to find a shape (*P*, 167).

Although the poet's ordering of words is conditioned by the language he hears and by the socio-economic world in which he lives,

---

[3] *Selected Essays of William Carlos Williams* (New York, 1954), p. 283. Hereafter cited as *SE*.

the poem does not write itself *through* the "passive Master," as
Emerson calls the artist. The poet is a maker, an inventor of form.
He is active, engaged in the world of experience, and the proper
form for the poem must be sought—painfully, laboriously—as the
poet attempts to achieve an order of words compatible with the
time, and language, flux in which he lives. This search is the major
theme of *Paterson*. While the poem may be considered from many
perspectives, the problem of form is a constant preoccupation of
the poet.

The everpresent river that flows through *Paterson*, filling our
ears with its falls (cadences) is literally the Passaic, but it is also
the flow of experience as reflected in the flow of consciousness. It
is also the stream of language, which rolls, "heavy with numbers."
The numbers represent the rhythm of the spoken language more
than the meters of the poetry of the past. It is in this spoken dialect that the poet must discover the measure of his verse. The
problem of finding a metrical form appropriate to the present age
has been commented upon by Williams: "We are trying . . . to seek
(what we believe is there) a new measure or a new way of measuring that will be commensurate with the social, economic world in
which we are living as contrasted with the past. It is in many ways
a different world from the past calling for a different measure"
(*SE*, 283). In the preface the author warns himself to "beware lest
he turn to no more than the writing of stale poems," following the
stereotyped patterns of the past.

While out of the river,

> . . . rolling up out of chaos,
> a nine months' wonder, the city
> the man, an identity—it can't be
> otherwise—an
> interpenetration, both ways . . . (*P*, 12)

These lines sum up the problem of establishing the relationship of
the society and the individual in appropriate language and measure. The search for form and the quest for identity are the same.
Neither the city, the poet, nor the poem is a self-sufficient entity.
They are interdependent elements of a cultural complex, and the
definition of any one involves interaction. The poet, as a man like
any other, may walk through the streets of an industrial New Jersey city, but both the city and he as an individual receive definition
only through the language of the poem, which is an abstraction
from the language that the poet has heard and read.

The discovery of identity requires the poet's understanding of his immediate, local environment and of his historical roots, including his language environment and his language roots. For Williams—with his vivid perception and his empathic responses—the question of *individual* identity often gets lost sight of:

> Why even speak of "I," he dreams, which
> interests me almost not at all? (*P*, 30)

This tendency to identify and merge helps to explain the shifts in point of view and in the personae of the protean narrator of the poem. The problem of identity and the problem of form are interrelated. The shifts complicate the poem; yet they are necessary. They are not capricious, but represent the poet's sensitivity to the problem of identity and of communication.

In Book I, which deals with the early history of Paterson as it defines the "elemental character of the place," the city, as the city of man, is linked with the as-yet-undiscovered identity of the poet. The river, which "comes pouring in above the city," is both the stream of history and of the individual life, as well as the stream of language from which the poet must derive his own speech:

> (What common language to unravel?
> ... combed into straight lines
> from that rafter of a rock's
> lip.)   (*P*, 15)

The failure of the language of the past is dramatized in the figures of Mrs. Sarah Cumming, "consort" of the Reverend Hopper Cumming, who died by a suicidal plunge into the falls during a sight-seeing excursion in 1812, and the daredevil Sam Patch, who began his career at Paterson and who died in a leap at the falls of the Genesee River in 1826. In these episodes, Williams uses prose to represent the language and character of the earlier time (not his own). The sentimentalized newspaper account of Mrs. Cumming's death ignores the reality of suicide and reflects the hypocrisy and the stifling gentility of the period. "A false language," the poet comments. As for Patch, the account of his reckless career and his final leap reveals the public's avidity for sensation and violence—empty marvels—but more particularly the substitution of unthinking action for meaningful speech. Williams has said that "the perfect type of the man of action is the suicide" (*SE*, 68). For both Mrs. Cumming and Patch society is an inhibiting force; and the final, desperate recourse of the individual blocked in an impulse toward genuine expression is an act of self-destruction. The failure of expression is indicated by the comment that in death both Mrs. Cumming and Patch are "silent, uncommunicative." The word *communicate*, negatived in such forms as *uncommunicative* and *incommunicado*, recurs throughout this part of the poem. It emphasizes the relation between communication and community and thus points up the lack of common values in Paterson, or any American city, from its beginnings, and the consequent waste and frustration of individual lives. A predicament shared by the poet.

Mrs. Cumming and Patch are only two of many instances of the warping influence of society in the early history of the falls community. Another is a "monster"—the hydrocephalic dwarf, Peter —like the falls, a celebrated and exploited "attraction" in Paterson. The dwarf's name is itself a link to the place and to the poet. The pattern of human life in this place, as in any other, is seen as "monstrous" and expressed in a deformed and corrupted language. In a note to Book I, Williams quotes from J. A. Symonds' *Studies of the Greek Poets* a passage describing the sprung verse of Hipponax as appropriate in view of "the harmony which subsists between crabbed verses and the distorted subjects with which they dealt—the vices and perversions of humanity . . ." (*P*, 53). The quotation reveals a preoccupation of Williams that complements his interest in the spoken language, and that is a rejection of traditional metrics in favor of a new measure, appropriate to the present, characterized by the "relativistic or variable foot" (*SL*, 335). Thus throughout *Paterson*, as throughout Williams' career, the quest for an appropriate form has involved the related problems of vocabulary, or diction, and measure, or "musical pace" (*SL*, 326).

Book II, "Sunday in the Park," presents the "modern replicas" of the life of the past. The park, "female to the city," brings the poet into contact with the immediate physical world, the sensual life which he must transform. In the park the Sunday crowd, the "great beast," takes its pleasures, pursues its desires among the "churring loves" of nature and in the sound of the voice of the evangelist who would bring them into the truth through the outworn language of the church, which the poet sees as simply another block to expression. Williams has elsewhere remarked that the church "is likely to be an insuperable barrier today if the major function of the artist—to lift to the imagination and give new

currency to the sensual world at our feet—is envisaged" (*SE*, 215).
In this constantly-changing, dying physical world, where

> The dogs and trees
> conspire to invent a world—gone! (*P*, 97)

no poet has come to create an adequate aesthetic world. Through
this scene the questing poet strolls as Faitoute, troubled by the
problem of inventing a poem commensurate with his world when
"the language is worn out." In his search, the poet rejects both the
crowd, the "beast," identified with unthinking sensuality, and the
conventional clichés of the mass society, as represented by the
evangelist. This necessitates the rejection of purely physical love
and reproduction as an end in itself. The denial is especially pain-
ful to this poet, who prizes the sensual life in which the poem must
begin. As he thinks of the voluptuous woman who is both his Muse,
offering the inspiration of the physical, and the Circe who would
enfold him and hold him in the web of the physical, the image that
begins in the sensual becomes transformed in his imagination:

> Her belly . her belly is like a white cloud . a
> white cloud at evening . before the shuddering night! (*P*, 105)

The poetic process involves an idealization of the physical, whereas
the purely physical life is sterile: "Stones invent nothing, only a
man invents." The river, as the purely sensual life, is a "terrifying
plunge, inviting marriage—and a wreath of fur" (*P*, 100). The
wreath of fur, a token of the obliteration of the human by the animal life (or the sinking of the individual human life into nature
through death, the plunge of Mrs. Cumming) is in powerful contrast to the conventional wreath of laurel, a "dead" image which
Williams has used as a base for his striking figure.

In Book III, "The Library," the poet turns from his immediate
world to the literature of the past in his search for a language and
a measure. Williams has described this stage of the quest as
"searching for a language (in books) and failing." [4] Confused by
the roar of events experienced in the park, the poet is attracted by
the "cool of books," which "sometimes lead the mind to libraries
of a hot afternoon" (*P*, 118). Turning over old newspaper files, he

---

[4] "*Notes:* Paterson III & IV . . . ," p. 32. Manuscript notebook in Abbott Collection, University of Buffalo Library.

is impressed by the failure of language to convey the meaning of
events:

> —a child burned in a field,
> no language. Tried, aflame, to crawl under
> a fence to go home. So be it. Two others,
> boy and girl, clasped in each others' arms
> (clasped also by the water) So be it. Drowned
> wordless in the canal. . . . (*P*, 120)

The violence and the failure of language parallel the examples of
Mrs. Cumming and Sam Patch in Book I, and in the poet's own
time they are paralleled by the violence and the failure of communication, and community, represented by the Paterson strikes.
The strikes, not dwelt on at length, remain in the background, a
brooding reminder of the violence and injustice of the social world.
Yet this violence is a part of the revolutionary process, the clearing
of the ground for a new order, a new measure, in society as well as
in art. The man on the picket line is, unknowingly, a brother of the
poet.

Seclusion in the library, at first a welcome retreat, breeds revul-
sion. The sound of books, the pressure of the past, becomes a roar
in the ears, threatening to be as overpowering as the flux of immediate experience. In contrast to the roar of the "wadded library," is the Beautiful Thing, sometimes personified as a woman,
to which the poet's mind drifts. This phrase, which recurs as a
kind of refrain, applies to the immediate physical world, which the
poet knows through his senses and out of which he makes poetry,
by invention, in a language appropriate to his experience: "The
province of the poem is the world" (*P*, 122). The Beautiful Thing,
which also harks back to the woman of Book II, is the inspiration
of this poet of the visible world.

The roar of the books, which is a part of the roar of the falls,
merges with the roar of "cyclone, fire, and flood," all actual events
in the history of Paterson. Metaphorically, however, these events
are involved in the creative process. The fire is poetic artifice for
Williams, just as it is for Yeats in "Sailing to Byzantium." The
creation of a poem, a new object, from the commonplace of life is
suggested by the image of an old bottle transformed by the fire:

> An old bottle, mauled by the fire
> gets a new glaze, the glass warped
> to a new distinction, reclaiming the
> undefined. (*P*, 142–143)

It is typical of the contrasting orientations of these two poets, re-flected in their diction and imagery, that Williams should select an object from ordinary life, a common vessel, while Yeats turns to the exotic mosaics and golden ornaments of the Byzantine arti-ficers.

The creative fire is a waterfall reversed, "shooting upward," as-serting a new reality, rather than subsiding in the anonymity of nature. The flame itself "surpasses heat" and the glass is splotched with rainbows of "cold fire" that attests the transmutation and distancing of experience in the poetic process. The fire destroys the literature of the past, just as the poet must reject its language to forge his own out of the living speech of the present. This is the revolutionary violence of art. The "vulgarity of beauty" of the beautiful thing surpasses all the perfections of the art of the past. It is a manifestation of immediate life and can be celebrated or expressed only by the contemporary poet. In this process the Beau-tiful Thing becomes

> intertwined with the fire. An identity
> surmounting the world, its core. . . . (*P*, 145)

But even so, the poet is aware of the inadequacy of his expression. "The words are lacking," the measures are lacking for an adequate representation of the Beautiful Thing (*P*, 146).

The actual flood is identified with the Biblical flood and with the almost overwhelming flood of language in which the poet is im-mersed. He rejects the language of the library (he cannot spend his life looking into the past). As he detaches himself, his perspective is described in the terms of the subsidence of an actual flood. The world is slimed with what may be a "fertile(?)mud," but which is at the same time a corrupt "pustular scum" giving forth a revolt-ing stench that "fouls the mind."

Attempting to re-order a world burdened by a false and dead language, the poet faces a problem of form:

> How to begin to find a shape—to begin to begin again,
> turning the inside out : to find one phrase that will
> lie married beside another for delight . ?
> —seems beyond attainment . (*P*, 167)

Recognizing the corruption of language, the poet asserts that the "words will have to be rebricked up," the language renewed, before an adequate form can be achieved. How long for such renewal?

—in a hundred years, perhaps—
the syllables
                    (with genius)
                        or perhaps
two lifetimes
Sometimes it takes longer . *(P, 171)*

In the meantime, what is the recourse of the poet standing by the river?

The past above, the future below
and the present pouring down: the roar,
the roar of the present, a speech—
is, of necessity, my sole concern . *(P, 172)*

Under the compulsion to make a "replica" of the falls, to invent a poem commensurate with his present reality, the poet can only find his meaning in the sliding water at the brink, where he must, as the opening of the poem suggested, "comb out the language," inadequate though his vocabulary and measure may seem, to give expression to whatever "episodes," or incomplete truths, he may have achieved in his lifetime.

Book IV, "The Run to the Sea," according to Williams' introductory note, is reminiscent of such episodes. The three subjects which this part of the poem introduces in succession are, first, love —of various kinds, each with its own frustrations—in the figure of a triangle involving a New York poetess (a Lesbian), a young nurse (the female Paterson and a Beautiful Thing), and the poet as Paterson; second, science, through the episode of a lecture on atomic fission to which Paterson takes his son (as an introduction to his heritage of the disruptive knowledge of his time); and third, money, as the cause of the concentration of capital and social corruption. These three topics all relate to the theme of divorce, alienation (the "sign of knowledge in our time"), first introduced in Book I; they are also intimately related to the problem of language. The question posed at the beginning of the third part of Book IV, "Haven't you forgot your virgin purpose, the language?" is intentionally misleading. The poet has been very much preoccupied with the problem of language in the preceding episodes.

Madame Curie's discovery of radium is cited in the discussion of science:

A dissonance
in the valence of Uranium

> led to the discovery
> Dissonance
> (if you are interested)
> leads to discovery (*P*, 207)

The radioactive energy released by the breaking down of the old element, uranium, represents not only the knowledge sought and achieved by the creative scientist but also poetic knowledge or truth. It is only through a breakdown of the old forms that the poet can hope to discover poetic truth for his time. The necessity of breaking down the old forms is supported by a reference to literature (Chaucer's Sir Thopas) as well as to science:

> Thy drasty rymyng is not
> worth a toord (*P*, 208)

There is a curative power in the energy released by the emergence of new forms ("a dissonance . . . may cure the cancer"). So too there is a restorative power in the poet's reworking of a corrupt language in his attempt to give expression to a "new culture." The same principle of renewal through the transmutation of a decaying order applies to love and economics within a society.

The last section of Book IV returns to an explicit concern for the problem of language. As the spent river winds slowly toward the sea, as the poet contemplates the waning of his own life, he comments on the need for leisure and detachment in his task: "Virtue . . . is a complex reward in all language, achieved slowly." In this phase the combing of the language, the experimentation with form, continues:

> Kill the explicit sentence, don't you think? and expand our meaning—by verbal sequences. Sentences, but not grammatical sentences: dead-falls set by schoolmen. Do you think there is any virtue in that? better than sleep? to revive us? (*P*, 222)

The breaking down of the formal sentence is in keeping with the abandonment of conventional meter in favor of the variable foot:

> She used to call me her
>   country bumpkin
> Now she is gone I think
>   of her as in Heaven
> She made me believe in
>   it . a little
> Where else could she go?   (*P*, 222)

As the river approaches the sea, of death, of unconscious nature into which the individual life merges, the assertion is made that the sea is *not* our home. The book ends with an image of renewal but not of rebirth in a religious or mystical sense. A figure is seen far out, swimming. First thought to be a duck or a dog (dogs as manifestations of the persistence of the instinctual life force abound in *Paterson*), the object proves to be a man, swimming toward the shore. On the beach, a large black dog, yawning and stretching, gets up to meet him as he emerges from the sea. After resting he gets up, slips into faded overalls, a shirt with rolled-up sleeves, and hat:

> Climbing the
> bank, after a few tries, he picked
> some beach plums from a low bush and
> sampled one of them, spitting the seed out,
> then headed inland, followed by the dog   (*P*, 238)

In his *Autobiography*, Williams comments on this episode: "In the end the man rises from the sea where the river appears to have lost its identity and accompanied by his faithful bitch, obviously a Chesapeake Bay retriever, turns inland toward Camden where Walt Whitman, much traduced, lived the latter years of his life and died. He always said that his poems, which had broken the dominance of the iambic pentameter in English prosody, had only begun his theme. I agree. It is up to us, in the new dialect, to continue it by a new construction upon the syllables." [5]

The sea in this context is not a symbol of rebirth and unity in the traditional sense of immortality for the poet and a perfectly-realized form for his work. It is rather the sea of nature, the sea of the mass of indifferent men, and the figure of the man emerging from the sea (the Odyssean wanderer or the Whitmanesque poet of the open road) represents both the new generation and the poet of *Paterson*. As a representative of a new generation, the figure can be identified with the young Paterson poet A. P., who has been writing to the narrator about his own problems of poetic form. The image is not so limited in its application, however. It includes not only the rising generation, but the aging poet himself, completing his poem, as one phase of his career, and rededicating himself to the continuing quest for a form which is never to be perfectly realized.

---

[5] *The Autobiography of William Carlos Williams* (New York, 1951), p. 392.

Seven years after the publication of *Paterson IV* and his *Auto-biography*—and shortly before the appearance of *Paterson V*—Williams again spoke of the ending of Book IV, commenting upon a change in the situation of the poet-protagonist: "*Paterson IV* ends with the protagonist breaking through the bushes, identifying himself with the land, with America. He finally will die but it can't be categorically stated that death ends *anything*. When you're through with sex, with ambition, what can an old man create? Art, of course, a piece of art that will go beyond him into the lives of young people, the people who haven't had time to create. The old man meets the young people and lives on." [6] It is fitting that the transition from Book IV to V be described as a breakthrough, because, while there is a continuity of image and theme and metrical form, there are significant differences in the poet's attitude and in the treatment of certain themes carried over from the earlier books.

The poet still calls himself Paterson, but he is less bound by his locality and his immediate present. A sense of freedom from time and place is asserted in the opening lines, in which even the visual contour of the verses is ideographic:

> In old age
> > the mind
> > > casts off
> > rebelliously
> > an eagle
> from its crag [7]

In this freedom there is a tendency to identify with man, or Western man, rather than with the citizens of Paterson past and present. The references to the city of Paterson are few. The falls, which sounded through the first four books, is not heard here. The only river specifically mentioned is the Ohio, with its falls at Louisville, below which Audubon, the artist-observer with whom the aging Paterson identifies, left his stranded boat to walk overland to his home at Henderson across three new states of the still-primitive continent.

There is also a greater concern for the past in *Paterson V*, not, as in the earlier books, in terms of its destructive and inhibiting

---

[6] *I Wanted to Write a Poem, the Autobiography of the Works of a Poet,* ed. Edith Heal (Boston, 1958), p. 22.

[7] *Paterson, Book Five* (New York, 1958), first page. Subsequent references in the text will be to *PF* and page, although in this edition the pages are unnumbered.

influences, but rather as a source of tradition in art that has sustained and guided the modern artist. The institution which represents the past, the art museum, is not rejected, as was the library in Book III:

> —the museum became real
> *The Cloisters*—
> on its rock
> casting its shadow—
> "la réalité! la réalité! . . . (*PF*, 3–4)

Paterson V is also a breakthrough in the sense that the roar of the falls, as it relates to the poet's struggle for recognition, is behind him. Paterson is more confident of his own position, although it is in no sense a terminus, and derives comfort from the fact that a world of art, of which he is a citizen, has through the years,

SURVIVED!

Reconciled with the past, he looks forward to the future, with which his own work is a link, and to the opportunity of helping younger poets in their efforts to master the poetic line. There is a continuation of the correspondence with the young poet introduced in Book IV as A. P. (Allen Paterson), with the difference that the younger man is here more clearly identified—and distinguished from the older Paterson—as A. G. (Allen Ginsberg).[8]

As for Williams' own line, there is a predominance of the staggered, breath-spaced metrical scheme that he first developed in Book II in the passage beginning,

> The descent beckons
> as the ascent beckoned
> Memory is a kind
> of accomplishment
> a sort of renewal. . . .   (*P*, 96)

In *Paterson V* this flexible form is efficiently adapted to the poet's needs. There is *not* the same emphasis upon the failure of communication, and expression, that marked the first four books.

In other respects, however, a continuity of theme is evident. The poet's concern for the Beautiful Thing persists—although the term is not used—and for its relation to artistic expression. There is,

---

[8] *Ibid.*, p. 7.

however, a greater assurance that the immediacy of experience, of the past as well as the present, is made available through art, as in the lyrics of Sappho; the *Nativity* of Peter Brueghel, the elder, "who painted what he saw"; and a medieval tapestry with its figure of a young woman waiting for her lover. In contrast, the only contemporary feminine representative of the Beautiful Thing is the figure of a woman in slacks who walks through the poet's town and with whom Paterson has been unable to establish contact. He is attracted, he desires, from a distance (of time as well as space), but there is no possibility of his establishing a relationship comparable even to the abortive romance with the nurse, Phyllis, in Book IV. Thus the theme of thwarted lust is continued, as are the themes of violence (war) and the corruption of the economic system (the latter supported by the inclusion of an unsigned letter, apparently from Ezra Pound). These themes are, however, less urgent than in the earlier parts of the poem.

The sense of frustration and dissatisfaction in the younger Paterson is opposed by the assurance that art can provide a release of blocked desire. The greatest frustration, of course, is death, or the sense of death, the "hole / in which we are all buried." There is an escape hatch, however, at the bottom of the hole, through the imagination, "which cannot be fathomed" (*PF*, 6).

The major conflict of Book V, as of the earlier poem, is still the tension between physical existence and the life of the imagination. But the demands of the libido are less formidable in advancing age. Just as the canine population of Paterson has dwindled, the "dog" of the poet's thoughts

> has shrunk
> to no more than a "passionate letter"
> to a woman, a woman he had neglected
> to put to bed in the past .   (*PF*, 24)

The letter, or art, provides a more satisfying outlet for physical desire than had formerly been the case.

His art, in which the poet now feels more secure, also provides a sense of community to relieve the alienation of earlier years. Just as the twelfth-century tapestry is the product of many hands following a common plan, working together,

> together as the cartoon has plotted it
> for them. All together ... (*PF*, 25–26)

so too the tradition of art with which the poet identifies himself represents a common endeavor, shared over the centuries. Besides Peter Brueghel, the elder, the roster includes Gertrude Stein, Paul Klee, Picasso, Juan Gris—all related to the development of modern abstract art, all artists concerned with movement and sensuous detail. Henri Toulouse-Lautrec, to whose memory *Paterson V* is dedicated, is the artist of the whore-house, the poet of the sensual life, which Williams values as the basis of art. The crippled Frenchman's election of the bordello is comparable to the American poet's embrace of the filthy Passaic in "The Wanderer." [9]

The most important and complex new image introduced in the new poem—and one which relates back to the earlier parts of the poem, particularly to the beast life of Book II—is the unicorn. This mythical creature with its animal shape and magical qualities synthesizes the physical life and the life of the imagination. It also serves as a synthesis of past and present, for in it are merged the European past (the wounded beast of the old tapestries), the primitive American past (the horned beast seen in the moonlight by Audubon on his long walk) and the poet's present situation, in which the "milk white one horned beast" is "penned by a low wooden fence," suggestive of the waning potency of age (*PF*, 26– 28). The unicorn is either a wounded victim (like the crippled painter) or a survivor of violent struggle, and he is identified with the artist. The beast also wears a collar. In the tapestry the beast surviving the hunt wears a "jeweled collar," while a hound he has gored lies nearby. The beast seen by Audubon lies wounded in a field,

> its neck
> circled by a crown!
> > from a regal tapestry of stars! (*PF*, 5)

Here the crown refers not so much to Audubon's claim to royal birth (the "Dauphin" legend) as to the achievement of the artist (essentially more noble) whose expression derives from the sensual life with its conflict and suffering.

These images are supported by Williams' description of the imagination escaping the trap of death, bearing

> . . . a collar round his neck
> hid in the bristling hair. (*PF*, 6)

---

[9] *The Complete Collected Poems of William Carlos Williams 1906–1938* (Norfolk, Conn., 1938), p. 312.

The image of the collared beast stands in brilliant contrast to the image of the wreath of fur in Book II. Whereas the wreath of fur invited a sinking into the anonymity of the beast life—an impulse rejected—the jeweled collar is the individual expression of the artist that distinguishes him from the beast. It is a badge of his identity and of his membership in a community, though a select one.

Through his measured expression the poet achieves the only reality he can ever know. This reality, figured as a dance, is dynamic and relative rather than static and absolute. The poet of *Paterson* concludes, or at least interrupts himself, on this note:

> We know nothing and can know nothing
> > but
> the dance, to dance to a measure
> contrapuntally,
> > Satyrically, the tragic foot. (*PF*, 33)

Satyrically, which punningly echoes the old confusion between *satire* and *satyr*, links the values of sensuality, the beast life, and art, as in the ancient drama with its chorus of satyrs. The reference to counterpoint as a necessary element of poetic form would seem to indicate not only the use of complementary and contrasting rhythmical patterns but also the tension between the physical and the imaginative life and correspondingly, in the language which expresses this conflict, between comparable and contrasting images (like the wreath of fur of Book II and the beast's collar of Book V).

The "measured dance" contains the poet's knowledge of reality, a knowledge which is relative and incomplete, rather than absolute. The dance of art, of knowledge, sustains the poet's imagination

> "unless the scent of a rose
> startle us anew"

as the claims of the immediate sensual life intervene (*PF*, 33). The dance, at any given time and place, is also a form which is tentative, straining toward completion, subject to change. In short, a dynamic, organic form.

Paterson, in either four or five parts, is a complex work, the form of which is difficult to appreciate. Yet it is honest and uncompromising (a reflection of the poet's mind). There is no suggestion of a wholeness dependent upon a systematized world view, or dialectic, where wholeness is intellectually indefensible. The failure of form resulting from the attempt to impose unity upon recalcitrant materials is illustrated by Hart Crane's *The Bridge*, the parts of which resist the false synthesis the poet sought to impose through force of will and which remains a collection of more or less brilliant poems.

Although Williams' work has received increasing critical attention, his search for an adequate and dynamic form has been productive to an extent not yet appreciated.[10] The range of his innovations in language and metrics will continue to be a rewarding subject. More important, his technical advances will undoubtedly be incorporated and projected in the work of poets to come. In this respect, Williams is like Whitman, whom he praises (with qualifications) for having broken through the "deadness of copied forms" (*SE*, 218). For Williams, every major work is seen as a beginning, and a continued, and a never-to-be-completed search for form. In his awareness of this quality of art, Williams also stands with Whitman, who in his 1855 preface wrote, "A great poem is no finish to a man or woman but rather a beginning. Has anyone fancied he could sit at last under some due authority and rest satisfied with explanations and realize and be content and full? To no such terminus does the greatest poet bring . . . he brings neither cessation or sheltered fatness and ease. The touch of him tells in action. Whom he takes he takes with firm sure grasp into live regions previously unattained . . . thenceforward is no rest. . . ." Williams also sees art as an ever-changing thing, productive of new forms to suit new occasions. He has spoken of the necessity of innovation and of being "at the advancing edge of art" as in the American tradition (*SL*, 142). He also looks forward to further development along the lines projected by the pioneers, himself included.

As for the publication of *Paterson Five*, following the supposedly-completed *Paterson* in four parts, Williams has explained the necessity of his expansion of the poem in a jacket note to the new volume: "After *Paterson, Four* ten years have elapsed. In that period I have come to understand not only that many changes have occurred in me and the world, but I have been forced to recognize that there can be no end to such a story I have envisioned with the terms which I had laid down for myself. I had to take the world of Paterson into a new dimension if I wanted to give it imaginative validity. Yet I wanted to keep it whole, as it is to me. . . ."

---

[10] More fully appreciated in 1970 than in 1960. (W. S.)

The "wholeness," or unity, of the poem is of course approximate rather than absolute, and it is conceivable that other books could be added to the poem, on Williams' terms, without violation of its status as a poetic whole. At any event, the appearance of *Paterson Five* is welcome evidence that Dr. Williams, at seventy-five, continues his eager quest for form.

Bernard Duffey

Williams' *Paterson* and the Measure of Art

Although William Carlos Williams is still insisted upon as a poet of things only, a poet of the noun, it seems more evident that the course of his poetry reflects a varying imbalance between the world and the poet's own mind. In many cases the weight swings in favor of the world. Imagist tenets have their way, and mind is subordinated to what it beholds. But "Objectivism" for Williams was a declaration of the poem's self-sufficiency [1] as well as its rooting in things, and sometimes, as in "The Yachts," there is a kind of stand-off in which mind at first effaces itself to serve as a sensing medium only but later reasserts creative independence at the expense of distorting, of making the world over in its own momentary image

Reprinted, with changes by the author, from *Essays on American Literature in Honor of Jay B. Hubbell,* ed. Clarence Gohdes (Duke University Press: Durham, N.C., 1967), 282–94, by permission of the Duke University Press and Bernard I. Duffey.

[1] Cf. the comment in his essay "Marianne Moore" in *Selected Essays* (New York, 1954), p. 125. "But what I wish to point [*sic*] is that there need be no stilled and archaic heaven, no ducking under religiosities to have poetry and to have it stand in its place beyond 'nature.' Poems have a separate existence uncompelled by nature or the supernatural. There is a 'special' place which poems, as all works of art, must occupy, but it is quite definitely the same as that where bricks or colored threads are handled."

and so producing a vision blurred between the two. Some poems are plainly didactic. Throughout, the pervading drama is that of idea, as theme or form, counterpointed against things. And nowhere is it more plain than in the first four books of *Paterson*.

A most elusive entity there is the reality of the central noun image itself. Town, mankind, poet, doctor, or the city's masses, the name's references shift again and again. The roar of the falls drowns out clear hearing just as their flood and spray forbid plain sight. Or the rush of the stream carries everything past and away before one can really see. Frederick Eckman has suggested the dominance of a verb rather than a noun effect in Williams, of motion and change rather than presence, and however this may be with the individual shorter poems, it exercises a strong power in *Paterson*.

Each of the first four books has a recurrent image of veiling or vanishing as its most obvious unifying force. In the first it is the stream of history containing the manifold events, the things of the poem. In the second there is the poet's walk through the park which brings more events and, especially, the evangelist whose sermon gushes forth a message of divine riches never realized outside the sadly ironic flow of its own sentiments. In the third book the Babel of the library is silenced only by the holocaust that seemingly burns up library and town alike, and, in the fourth, personal disintegration is matched by atomic and economic breakdown and apparent death in the sea except for a lone swimmer who makes an ambiguous way to shore and his future: but, "the future's no answer," declares the poet, "I must/find my meaning—or succumb." [2]

If there is no answer in the future, there is only a hazy reality in past or present. Williams' "things" in *Paterson* are very sparse in themselves, insubstantial and inherently unsuggestive of much except surface characteristics. In this they resemble objects in his shorter poems. Locust trees, snow lying on the ground, workmen or idlers, lakes, spring shoots, an old woman eating plums, fountains, multitudinous birds, flowers, and plants, and images of the poet himself pop up and down in a verse where the charm of everything lies in the moment rather than in dominating presence or dwelt-

[2] *Paterson* (New York, [1963]), p. 173. In future references to Williams's work the following abbreviations will be used: *P, Paterson; CEP, Collected Early Poems* (New York, [1951]); *CLP, Collected Later Poems* (revised edition; New York, [1963]); *PB, Pictures from Breughel* (New York, [1962]); *SE, Selected Essays* (New York, 1954); *SL, Selected Letters* (New York, [1957]); *W, I Wanted to Write a Poem* (New York, 1958).

upon actuality. To look at one of the shorter poems by itself is, most often, like looking at a sketch whose detail, relations, and import are only tentatively suggested, and to read through a group of the shorter poems is to experience a *perpetuum mobile* (in the phrase Williams twice used as a title) not very unlike reading *Paterson* itself.

Despite his occasional parallels to Joyce, the town of Paterson is not a Dublin for the American. A falls, a bridge, a park, industry (generalized), occasional buildings or streets, these are most of what we get of the city in an effect vastly different from the Dublin of *Ulysses* and different even more from the Dublin, or the rivers, of *Finnegans Wake* where things and ideas are without question bound to each other in words alone. Williams is an impressionist, simplifying language, using it to catch onto a few flamboyant shapes and colors for whatever immediate arrest of attention compels him. But he is also an impressionist with a message, and as a result his poem grows into an argument. It posits ideas, supplies examples, and draws conclusions.

It would not be outrageously paradoxical to suggest of *Paterson* I–IV that it presents few things but in ideas, that it is the forms themselves of meaningless flux, unreal stasis, and the poet's despair of language which are really the generative force for his images. In Book One, Part I, for example, the people associated with Paterson are set forth as automatons, and as automatons they are made to act, "Who because they/neither know their sources nor the sills of their/disappointments walk outside their bodies aimlessly/for the most part" (*P*, 14). The second part of Book One then contemplates history as a possible source of meaning but rejects it because such learning rejects experience: "Divorce is/the sign of knowledge in our time/divorce! divorce!" (*P*, 28), and there follow some dozen images of divorce. In the third part, argument is raised a degree into allegory, but earth as the "father of all speech" is seen only dimly under the flood of false speech and false learning which enshrouds him.

The poem is not so much lyric or epic as it is a book of parables showing mind and will fallen from a sovereign place in the kingdom of experience. Sister M. Bernetta Quinn has seen *Paterson* as the expression of idealistic mind denied its office. "In the Word alone is life," she notes, referring to logos as reason or thought, "and the contemporary Paterson feels that Word to be inaccessible." Williams' imagination cannot really trust things here despite its affirmations to itself because it cannot find itself reflected in

them. It can only behold their existence outside itself. The result
is unhappiness apprehended as a sense of poetic failure: one suggested by the "lame or limping iambics" (*P*, 53) cited from John
Addington Symonds at the end of Book One; by the sardonic self-
injunction toward the end of Book Two, "Go home. Write. Compose./Ha!/Be reconciled, poet, with your world, it is/the only
truth!/Ha!/—the language is worn out" (*P*, 103); by the distant
comfort, "in a hundred years, perhaps—/the syllables," (*P*, 171)
at the end of Book Three; or by the nostalgic cry of Book Four,

> Oh that the rocks of the Areopagus had
> kept their sounds, the voices of the law!
> Or that the great theater of Dionysius
> could be aroused by some modern magic
>   to release
> what is bound in it, stones!
> that music might be wakened from them to
> melt our ears.
>   (*P*, 235)

Paterson, in these passages and many like them, takes a place in
that long line of laments for failed imagination heralded by
Coleridge's "Dejection, an Ode" or, in America, by Poe's "Israfel."

The subject of *Paterson* I–IV is not things, though these are its
occasions. It is rather the dejection of the idealistic imagination,
conning one more time its own inability to raise the show of things
to the desires of the mind. I am suggesting, thus, my agreement
with those views of the poem which have seen its unity as one
essentially of parallel themes developed by examples, though the
same argument may also suggest that it is too long, that its whole
substance is brought into view well before its conclusion. Certainly
the parallelisms forward this recognition. As history can redeem
nothing in Book One, neither can religion in Book Two, the library
or the fire in Book Three, or the world of science or economics in
Book Four. None of these is of use within the world of Paterson
itself, or to the poet's search for his language, and their failure becomes increasingly predictable as the poem unfolds.

Paterson I–IV presents no alternative to failure. Elsewhere, in
verses like "The Botticellian Trees" or "Burning the Christmas
Greens," the subject had undergone a change natural to its cir-
cumstances, and one in which the poet found progress and form.
Coherence lay in natural change itself. In his poem titled "Lear"
Williams wrote about such trust in the nature of things:

> When the world takes over for us
> and the storm in the trees
> replaces our brittle consciences
> (like ships female to all seas)
> when the few last yellow leaves
> stand out like flags on tossed ships
> at anchor—our minds are rested.
>
> (*CLP*, 237)

To set *Paterson* I–IV off against these more integral uses of what Mrs. Linda Wagner calls the "transitional metaphor," against poems whose meaning is a reflection of natural process in its human aspect, suggests an important but shifting operation of the pathetic fallacy. "The Botticellian Trees" welcomes the trees' change from winter bareness to summer opulence as a metamorphosis of abstract language into full reality and of male into female. In such a poem the world does take over for the poet and for us and, in doing so, forms the poem. *Paterson* I–IV, in turn, operates on a middle but not very happy ground created by the discovery and multiplication of elements decisively foreign or hostile to the mind's desires, an alien or blank process inaccessible to understanding or fellow feeling, capped by the totally unassimilable image of the sea "which is *not* us."

Williams occasionally reaches something like a third condition, suggested perhaps in "Choral: The Pink Church," where the poet's mind attempts to accept outright its own idealistic loyalties. The poetic cost of this third phase is great, however. To celebrate abstract loyalties in a verse designed to cope with concrete and personal experience is to risk a variety of failures, and "The Pink Church," along with *Paterson* I–IV, achieves its share. One is confusion of meaning as the abstract and concrete awarenesses jostle against each other:

> Sing!
> transparent to the light
>   through which the light
> shines, through the stone,
>   until
> the stone light glows,
>   pink jade
> —that is the light and is a stone
> and is a church—if the image
>   hold . . .
>
> (*CLP*, 159–160)

I think it doubtful that the image does hold in this case, and that such failure of fusion parallels the incoherence of *Paterson* I–IV, an inability to raise the pathetic fallacy; here to put light and stone together and by them suggest something out of nature properly discernible as a church. Another risk, when the poem leaves nature out, is stridency and sloganizing. Or, when the poem at its close bears down on poetic and political positions without exactly depending on them, there is the risk of a smudged invocation of party lines—dimming them to an even remoter degree of abstraction than their original one:

> Joy! Joy!
> —out of Elysium!
> —chanted loud as a chorus from
>   the Agonistes—
> Milton, the unrhymer,
>   singing among
>   the rest . . .
>   like a Communist
>   (*CLP,* 162)

Perhaps "The Pink Church" strives for what Theodore Roethke once admired under the name of "sophisticated looniness," but it also strives for rather heavy spiritual affirmation, and the two aims clash. There is no container for them, no single medium within which they can work together.

Such, at any rate, is the suggestion of *Paterson* V (1958) and the poems collected in *Pictures from Breughel* (1962) as they turn away from nature and abstract ideas to draw a large share of their themes and images from music, painting, and other literature. Glauco Cambon has suggested that *Paterson* I–IV had washed itself clean of aestheticism in the dirty Passaic, but the later poems affirm a new-found dependence, a newly discovered parent imagination in art. Such a change in content is paralleled by Williams's growing concern with "measure," most immediately the rhythm of his own verse as experimentation carried him toward a degree of regular form in the "variable foot." But metrical concern is only one expression of the larger idea defined in capital letters and italics at the beginning of *Paterson* V.

> "What has happened to Paris
> since that time?
>   and to myself"?
> A WORLD OF ART

THAT THROUGH THE YEARS HAS
SURVIVED!
(*P,* 243–244)

And, as Book Five progresses, it seems clear not only that a world
of art has survived, but that it has come to heal the nature-mind
divorce symbolized in Books I–IV. The composite Paterson van-
ishes out of the poem except for a single reference, and the word
otherwise is used only to mean the poet himself. In place of its
earlier associations comes another kind of catalogue. There is
Toulouse-Lautrec, to whom the poem is dedicated, who made his
own kind of wittily redeeming measure. He is followed by Lorca,
the Unicorn tapestry of the Cloisters (which becomes a new central image), Philippe Soupault, Audubon, Jackson Pollock, Ben
Shahn, Ezra Pound, Mezz Mezzrow, the dance (a second extended
image), Gertrude Stein, Paul Klee, Arabic art, Dürer, Leonardo,
Bosch, Picasso, Juan Gris, Beethoven, and Breughel himself. Most
of these become examples of the artist's power to make the world
his home whether it be in Toulouse-Lautrec's brothels or Jackson
Pollock's world of pure paint.

This particular use of art to the poet is suggested in the excerpt
he includes in *Paterson* V from an interview with Mike Wallace. As
he uses art to reshape his own world, he eases himself away from
the starkness of encounter prevailing in the earlier work and dis-
covers the possibility of a poetry sufficient to itself as it is sufficient
to its creator and independent of "things."

Q. Mr. Williams, can you tell me, simply, what poetry is?
A. Well ... I would say that poetry is language charged with
   emotion. It's words, rhythmically organized. ... A poem is a
   complete little universe. It exists separately. Any poem that
   has worth expresses the whole life of the poet. It gives a view
   of what the poet is. (*P,* 261)

One can only guess how aware Williams may have been of his combined use and alteration of Pound's formula, "language charged
with meaning" to "language charged with emotion." But the formula in itself suggests his awareness of shifting from the pragmatic
and mimetic intent of the earlier parts of the poem to an expressive
one, of abandoning the outright reconciling of people with stones
for the different and more congenial function of creativity, declared and exhibited as such. The change does not remake *Paterson,* but it eases the overwhelming burden of Books I–IV, the

stark, unaided effort at harmonizing mind and the jumble of cir-
cumstance.

To recognize art as an act only of imagining and forming within
mind itself is to liberate creativity from impossible tasks. This
Kant-like doctrine is at the center of Williams's new awareness.
As the transcendental aesthetic was for Kant a freedom obtainable
without affecting the real limits of pure or practical reason, so
Williams's imagination, on the evidence of art, is a freedom of mind
attainable within a world defined by idea and experience. Art does
not become a means of special knowledge. It does become the area
within which mind can exercise itself in the limits and attainments
of its own measuring nature. Williams made this explicit in a letter
of 1955 to John C. Thirlwall.

> But in the arts, the art of the poem, lie resources, which when we
> become aware of their existence make it possible for us to liberate
> ourselves, or so I believe and think. . . .
> The first thing you learn when you begin to learn anything about
> this earth is that you are eternally barred save for the report of
> your senses from knowing anything about it. Measure serves for
> us as the key; *we can measure between objects; therefore we know
> they exist.* Poetry began with measure, it began with the dance,
> whose divisions we have all but forgotten. . . . (*SL,* 330–332, *pas-
> sim, italics added*)

Pictures from Breughel, from the title poems on, is largely an
exploration out and into this sense of poetry, the plainest token of
which is its frequent return to art objects as touchstones of accomplished thought or feeling. With great frequency, it achieves
through them the junctures whose failure was the burden of the
first four books of *Paterson.* "How shall we get said what must be
said?" Williams asks in "The Desert Music" (*PB,* 108–109). The
question is familiar in its repetition, but there is now an answer.

> Only the poem.
>
> Only the counted poem, to an exact measure:
> to imitate, not to copy nature, not
> to copy nature
>
> NOT, prostrate, to copy nature
>   but a dance! to dance
>
> two and two with him—
>
>   sequestered there asleep,
>   right end up!
>   (*PB,* 108–109)

Whether the sleeping Mexican of "The Desert Music" is like the sleeping Paterson, or, being "right end up," different, Williams's lines here find an Aristotelian formula of parallel measure between nature and art that declares creation to be possible.

The metrical experimentation that had marked all his work continues on into this poetry of the last two volumes, and the poems themselves continue to function as associative wholes, but they gain a new framework for association. "Measure," here, goes beyond metrics to relate poetry to a perennial creative enterprise, and personal association is given an impersonal backing. Williams's sparrow still cries out lustily, but his crying is "a trait/more related to music/than otherwise" (*PB*, 129), and his "image/is familiar as that of the aristocratic/unicorn" (*PB*, 130). A woman fussing with her hair is a "classic picture" (*PB*, 142), and the hitherto intractable sea calls to mind "the *Iliad*/and Helen's public fault/that bred it" (*PB*, 158). Through measure, our experience of it combined with a constant imagining of it, even the sea may be taken into account, for art and life both.

> There is no power
>   so great as love
>   which is a sea,
>
> which is a garden—
>   as enduring
>   as the verses
>
> of that blind old man,
>   destined
>   to live forever
>   (*PB,* 166)

These lines are an associative sequence almost exactly like the first of my quotations from "The Pink Church," but their allusion to Homer puts an image of achieved and admirable order-in-chaos between the pattern of nature and the pattern of feeling instead of leading from nature through personal feeling to a largely wishful postulation of order. Personal acts of discovery need not bear the form of the poem, or its truth, by themselves. Homer has written of the power of love and of the sea, and his verses, which are like a garden, can be invoked by the poet as the defining part of an environment.

Williams had discovered a kind of allusion useful to his poetry as Pound's and Eliot's had been to theirs. Before about 1950 two Americans had lain heavily in his awareness. With Walt Whitman he acknowledged somewhat grudgingly a sense of shared dilemma, and he had taken Poe's radical loneliness as prototypical of American poetry. But the later work indicates a change. Poetry is still to be of his own time and place, but these, unlike Whitman's vision of himself especially, are included in a contemporary world of art. In the idea of art things and thoughts (still existing to themselves) can be seen integrally, under an aspect of contemplation rather than estrangement. Williams's sense of art is more like Poe's, though it is much more richly furnished. In it the idealistic imagination can live freely as it cannot do in the realm of pure fact.

Art works poetically for Williams like a recasting of nature, or the finding of a second nature, of something to "take over for us" in the failure of mind's power to reclaim its alienation. It is thus more an aspect of poetic relation than any advance into new language or new values as such. Paterson shrinks from his somewhat pretentious vagueness into the one form that had always really been his, that of the poet's perception seeking peace with itself. What the exercise of the pathetic fallacy or of moral idealism had failed to sustain, the power of a comparing, measuring imagination might accomplish. Imagination comes to see the need and use of a harmony to be achieved in imagination itself. This is, for example, the idea of later love poems like "The Ivy Crown" and "Asphodel, That Greeny Flower." Their whole substance is imagination conceived as the fabric of love.

> Medieval pageantry
> is human and we enjoy
> the rumor of it
>
> as in our world we enjoy
> the reading of Chaucer,
> likewise
>
> a priest's raiment
> (or that of a savage chieftain).
> It is all
>
> a celebration of the light.
> All the pomp and ceremony
> of weddings,
>
> "Sweet Thames, run softly
> till I end
> my song,"—
> Are of an equal sort.
>   (*PB,* 181)

And whatever of sharp encounter may be lacking in this later poetry is to be compensated for by something at last discovered and adhered to.

> Light, the imagination
> and love
> in one age,
>
> by natural law,
> which we worship,
> maintain
>
> all of a piece
> their dominance
> (*PB,* 180)

Here the figure of light means something like sensation or experience, imagination the measuring or comparing activity of art, and love the fruit of the two. Under this total aspect, experience can be conceived freely and in an achieved relation.

Is such an idea too sentimental, the retreat of an old and ailing man into cliché? On some occasions it can sound that way. The figure of the dance, as Hugh Kenner noted in his review of *Paterson, Book V*, seems all too available, but the idea of dance had been one of Williams's earliest as well as one of his later ideas of art. He had made the claim as early as *Kora in Hell*, and repeated it throughout the pages of that volume of 1920. Speaking against the simile, urging the need for sensing particulars as such, he yet maintained a need for imagined relation, for measure.

> All is confusion, yet it comes from a hidden desire for the dance.
>
> But one does not attempt by the ingenuity of the joiner to blend the tones of the oboe with the violin. On the contrary, the perfection of the two instruments is emphasized by the joiner; no means is neglected to give to each the full color of its perfections. It is only the music of the instruments which is joined, and that not by the woodworker but by the composer, by virtue of the imagination.
>
> On this level of the imagination all things and ages meet in fellowship. Thus only can they, peculiar and perfect, find their release. This is the beneficent power of the imagination. (*SE,* 15)

And *Kora* was "the one book I have enjoyed referring to more than any of the others," Williams said. "It reveals myself to me" (*W,* 26).

In the place of simile, too bindingly explicit an analogy, Williams this early postulated the freer measuring activity of art figured here as dance or the shifting relation of discrete things. His idea was certainly not very different in theory or practice from Pound's "superimposition" of images. But the measure of art, the patterning of complementary or contrasting images, contained a principle of poetic self-sufficiency which over the years of his writing Williams had mixed with the pathetic fallacy or with even more outright thematic principles like those of "The Pink Church." In such cases, the poem inhered partly in the measure of art, or the free shaping of images, and partly in the assertion of ideas. *Kora in Hell*, perhaps, revealed more of the poet to himself as it, more than any other text, allowed for a free dance of mind in relation to its objects.

Dance reappeared briefly in Williams' next volume, *Sour Grapes* (1921), in "Overture to a Dance of Locomotives."

> Gliding windows. Colored cooks sweating
> in a small kitchen. Taillights—
>
> In time: twofour!
> In time: twoeight!
> —rivers are tunneled: trestles
> cross oozy swampland: wheels repeating
> the same gesture remain relatively
> stationary: rails forever parallel
> return on themselves infinitely.
>   The dance is sure
>   (*CEP,* 195)

Here again the figure asserted is freedom to organize the descriptive detail of the train in motion according to a free selection and patterning of details, images juxtaposed like those of a cinematic montage. In *Spring and All* (1923), Neil Myers has argued, the theme itself of the volume is to be found in its shattering of the "natural" image in favor of new and cubistic designs. Certainly the awakening force of spring in "On the Road to the Contagious Hospital," the poem opening the sequence, is measured off not only against the equally asseverant forces of disease implied in the title but also against the "pink confused with white" of a pot of flowers in the poem which follows. The same measure continues into poem three where "the artist figure of/the farmer" stands in early spring "composing" his fields against their natural inclination to wilderness.

Paterson I–IV, unlike these works, had been shaped in what might be called the mixed mode of Williams's composition. Its assertive logical core was an explicitly developed essay on the poet's difficulties with a world of experience to which none of the analogies for poetry available to him seemed very congruent, and it also contained an abundance of imagery. But though some of this latter seemed patterned according to its own inherent suggestiveness, more lay under control by the theme. *Paterson* V changed the theme to assert the measure of art as an aesthetic idea stemming from the "WORLD OF ART/THAT THROUGH THE YEARS HAS SURVIVED." The sensuous and aesthetic was saved from its own dissolution by being made explicitly into a world of its own reference sufficient to itself as a mode of order. Art survives where nothing else has. The measure of art became the highest organization of human experience, the genetrix of beauty, and of comprehension, freedom, and love.

Williams's measure of art was a relation of things sufficient to its creator, one discerned despite Things' failure to speak a logical or pragmatic relationship in themselves. It was a marriage ritual of otherwise separate or fleeting impressions. Imagining the sea as a garden by virtue of its likeness to Homer's poetry would be truer to art than rejecting the sea flatly as chaos, because such measuring *was the idea of art*. The poet, Williams had told Mike Wallace, makes his own world, and he now declared the principle by which such a world could be made.

Williams's late poetry could achieve few if any unconditional victories over experience, but that effort had been the weakness of "The Pink Church" as despair of it had plagued the first four books of *Paterson*. What was needed more, in any case, was the forming of objects for the mind so that the mind need not instantly be defeated by them and so of avoiding the fool's mate of despair. The measure of art was the practice of an aesthetic freedom among the given particulars of nature. And now, beyond that, it became the aesthetic principle itself validated by the world of art within which the poet had grown.

Linda Wagner

A Bunch of Marigolds

I have been ill, as you perhaps have heard. This is the second time I have been knocked out. But this time I seem to have come out of it with a clearer head. Perhaps it derived from a feeling that I might have died or, worse, have been left with a mind permanently incapacitated. That it has not happened is a piece of pure good fortune. As a result of the enforced idleness and opportunity for thought, it may be, I have brought hard down on the facts of a situation which can no longer be delayed in the bringing of it to a final summary. I must now, in other words, make myself clear. I must gather together the stray ends of what I have been thinking and make my full statement as to their meaning or quit.

....What will come of my "idleness," which has been forced on me by my illness, it is hard to say. Will I be able to maintain it? I should passionately like to use it for the further development of my reading and my thinking and my doing if I can. I don't want to go back to the practice of medicine. The opportunity to complete my task as poet has never seemed so hopeful and attractive as now. (*William Carlos Williams to Louis Martz, May 27, 1951*)

The later poetry of William Carlos Williams, that written from approximately 1950 to 1963, provides remarkable evidence of the poet's steady technical accomplishment. More important, perhaps, even in these days of the carefully crafted poem, is the pervasive tone of surety, of contentment, that is the keystone of Williams' later work. The angry younger man of the '30s—who turned from poems to short stories in the midst of his acute personal depression —had come to realize that private satisfactions are greater than public ones, that his own happiness (finding it when and where he could) was more important than the condition of the world surrounding him. Let me not be misunderstood: Williams, even in old age, could never be termed "mellow." He was still displeased, still reproving, still irate—at times. He had, however, found many things in which to rejoice.

Reprinted from *The Kenyon Review,* XXIX (1967), 86–102, by permission of *The Kenyon Review* and Linda Wagner.

As the opening quotation shows, one of Williams' greatest pleasures lay in his power to create. Despite the warm defense in his *Autobiography* of the compatibility between medicine and poetry, he felt the need ultimately to concentrate on poetry. To live with a mind free from a doctor's responsibilities was a new and gratifying experience. He sounds almost pleased that his health was forcing him into "retirement," a retirement that was timely, too, so far as his poetry was concerned.

Williams had recently completed the fourth book of *Paterson,* an epic he was later to term an "experiment," "a restudy of the poetic line." He had begun the long poem in the early '40s (though he had thought about it often prior to that time)—significantly, following a three-year period of stalemate. The kinds of poems he had written earlier—vivid and satisfying as the best of them are —were no longer capable of expressing what he felt compelled to say. So he turned to the new experience of a *Paterson*, a poem much broader, much richer than anything he had ever before attempted. The differing techniques used within the first four books are proof of his search for new, more effective expression. It is, then, in some ways strangely opportune that his physical breakdown occurred at a point in time when his poetic invention had brought him to new areas of creativity. For these reasons, I consider the "later" work to date from 1950. Such poetry has the benefit of a decade of active experimentation during the '40s, and of a concentration never before possible in Williams' lifetime.

Worksheets from the last decade of his writing show that the great change in his life brought a noticeable modification in his methods of writing. Later poems like "Suzy" (included in *Pictures from Brueghel*) have perhaps ten different versions, content changing as radically as does line arrangement. The final stanzas of "Suzy" describe the grandfather-poet's love for the girl, his deeply protective feelings about her. Yet, in earlier versions, the grandfather was scarcely mentioned. Attention was given instead to a mysterious older woman, with the poet partaking in a kind of worship rather than in an immediate relationship with his granddaughter.

Final Version of Part III
a bunch of violets clutched
in your idle
hand gives him a place

beside you which he cherishes
his back turned
from you casually appearing

not to look he yearns after
you protectively
hopelessly wanting nothing

Intermediate Version	*Earliest Version*
there the smiling image of	beyond which will be
an old man slaps	a woman of
his thigh Suzy the image	awe inspiring presence
changes to a woman of	Suzy before whom both
awe inspiring	the old man
beauty from both our dreams	and yourself will join
in whose historic worship	gripping hands
we join our hands	agape trembling sweating
open mouthed in praise	in grudging praise

Worksheets for Williams' earlier poems were, for the most part, quite close to the finished poem. He may have revised, but his revisions were usually one of two kinds: deletions of entire lines or passages, or rearrangements of words within lines. There is seldom the rethinking, the recasting, that one finds in the worksheets of poems contained in *Pictures from Brueghel.* Mrs. Williams has said also that Williams worked much more carefully late in his life. His last play, *The Cure*, for example, was planned—and the plan dictated to Mrs. Williams—while they were visiting with friends. Dr. Williams actually wrote the play only after they had returned home. As a rule, his earlier writing had been done as he thought of it, without preliminary notes or outlines.

Physical impairment was doubtless responsible for some of the change in Williams' working pace: he could type or write only with his left hand. His activity of necessity was slower. Perhaps these changes also influence the new tone of tranquility in many of the poems. Perhaps they are immaterial.

At best, the fact that Williams' method of working had to be adjusted is only of secondary importance in a consideration of his late poems. Their aura of contentment, of joy seems to me their most distinctive quality—an impression achieved partly through stately pace, but more emphatically through content. Whether Williams muses with some sadness about the neighbor he has never visited, or describes wryly the "young woman/on whose belly I have never/slept though others/have," he is happy. There is no question about the hard-won contentment that brings him to write the tender "To Asphodel, That Greeny Flower." When he writes lovingly of his poetry—as he does in "The Desert Music" and *Paterson* V—or of his grandchildren—in "Three Stances," "Suzy," and "Paul"—Williams is a man at peace with himself.

J. Hillis Miller has pointed out that many of Williams' late poems deal with death. But even here, as a rule, there is tranquility. Only rarely does he rage against the inevitable. More often he affirms the power of love, as in "The Rewaking" ("and so by/your love the very sun/itself is revived") or in "Asphodel," where he declares of love that "Death/is not the end of it." On occasion, he assumes the practical attitude of the old goose described so well in "To Daphne and Virginia."

> there, penned in,
>   or he would eat the garden,
>   lives a pet goose who
> tilts his head
>   sidewise
>   and looks up at us,
> a very quiet old fellow
>   who writes no poems.
>   Fine mornings we sit there
> while birds
>   come and go.
>   A pair of robins
> is building a nest
>   for the second time
>   this season. Men
> against their reason
>   speak of love, sometimes,
>   when they are old. It is
> all they can do
>   or watch a heavy goose
>   who waddles, slopping
>   noisily in the mud of
>   his pool.

As Williams depicts it, one feels that old age is something to respect; that it brings wisdom and, with it, a slow coda of renewed, renewing love.

He seems newly aware not only of his wife and family, and of the place of death in his life, but also of man as an admirable being. His early poems often berated men, though seldom so vituperatively as the Sacco and Vanzetti poem, "Impromptu: The Suckers." Early sections of *Paterson*, too, appear negative because they focus on the undesirable human being. The tone of the epic is alleviated, however, by the implication that, in contrast, good men do exist—as in the picnic scene when Mary cajoles her younger companions:

> Come on! Wassa ma'? You got
> broken leg? . . .
>
> —lifts one arm holding the cymbals
> of her thoughts, cocks her old head
> and dances! raising her skirts:
>
> La la la la!
>
> What a bunch of bums! Afraid somebody see
> you?
> Blah!
> Excrementi!
> —she spits.
> Look a' me, Grandma! Everybody too damn
> lazy.

For the most part, Williams' later poems emphasize the good of mankind, perhaps partly because, as he writes in "The Gift," "All men by their nature give praise./It is all/they can do."

In the poems of *The Desert Music, Journey to Love, Paterson* V, and *Pictures from Brueghel*, Williams turns for inspiration to people he loves. And he loves them for somewhat different reasons from those of Williams the younger poet. The 1944 poem "To Ford Madox Ford in Heaven" praised Ford for his ability to "roust and love and dredge the belly full." In 1955, Williams praises his wife of "Asphodel" for her ability to embody love:

> It was the love of love,
>   the love that swallows up all else,
>   a grateful love,
> a love of nature, of people,
>   animals,
>   a love engendering
> gentleness and goodness
>   that moved me
>   and *that* I saw in you . . .

Perhaps some insight into Williams' later attitudes can be gained by his clearer emphasis on the "irrational," a term which would have fitted awkwardly into the objectivist principles of the 1930s. Under that rationale, only factual presentations were valid. The artist as persona was to be nonexistent. Yet, by 1951, Williams had written to one of the critics he most admired, Sister M. Bernetta Quinn, that the weakness of many modern compositions is their failure to include the irrational. "In life (you show it by your tolerance of things which you feel no loss at not understanding) there is much that men exclude because they do not understand. The truly great heart *includes* what it does not at once grasp, just as the great artist includes things which go beyond him."

It is this same vein of thinking that leads Williams to recognize and applaud the strength of Dylan Thomas' poetry: not reason but heart, not logic but love.

> ... this is impassioned poetry, you might call it drunken poetry, it smacks of the divine—as Dylan Thomas does also.
>
> The analytic spirit that might have made him backtrack and reconsider, building a rational system of thought and technique, was not his. He had passion and a heart which carried him where he wanted to go. . .

The issue of Williams' later poetry—both its attitudes and technical qualities—is important for several reasons. First, it seems to be a given today that poets weaken in ability toward the end of their careers. In Williams' case, however, his later writing is strong. For the first time in his career, continuity and evenness are evident in his performance. The work of his last decade can be judged both as a whole and as a fitting apex for his writing of the previous forty years. The error of those critics who tried to find such culmination in *Paterson*, Books I through IV, can now be rectified: *Paterson* I–IV was further experimentation. *Paterson* V, in contrast, is a part of the climactic work. It is of little interest whether Williams' late work is consistently good because he had time for increasing revision, or because he had long since mastered the craft of poetry. Perhaps both statements are true. What *is* of interest is that the late poetry must be counted, not ignored, as it has recently been.

Second, recognition of Williams' late poetry is important because of an increasing tendency to see him as a disillusioned artist, a man defeated by his time and its people. Karl Shapiro speaks of *Paterson* as an "abandonment" of all Williams' poetic principals; Richard Gustafson calls the work a "tragedy." Bernard Duffey finds a growing pessimism, a decided withdrawal, in the late poems. David Ignatow speaks of Williams' hesitation, his bewilderment, his defeat. Each of these people admires Williams; each is saddened at the thought that the great champion of poetry as an American art was beaten, finally, by the very situation he had once worshipped.

The time has come to re-evaluate arguments for this point of view. The most pervasive appears to be the "change" in Williams' definition of his "local." According to this argument, for forty years Williams taught that a man's surroundings were the only valid source for his imaginative work, that a man had to know his local intimately in order to re-create it, or any of the phases of life apparent in it. The old woman munching on plums, the wind-blown brown paper, the sprig of Queen Anne's lace—all are segments of Williams' local. However, say these readers, Williams' last three books of poetry are different. Not only is a whole sequence of poems based on graphic art—Brueghel's paintings—but there is frequent mention of music, drama, other poetry, other art objects. The green glass between hospital walls represented, for them, Williams' "real" local. These later poems are, they contend, making use of "traditional" references—literary, unreal, un-local.

One could answer this assumption in several ways. To see the worn, white-covered collection of Brueghel's paintings lying prominently on Williams' bookcase is to realize that the prints of which he writes *are* a part of his immediate local, a local defined by him in this 1944 discussion of art (in a letter to Horace Gregory):

> If, as I believe and keep always before my eyes, if art is a transference—for psychic relief—from the actual to the formal, and if this can only be achieved by invention, by rediscovery, by reassertion by the intelligence and the emotions in any and every age —and if the grand aspect of this living drive is, when it occurs, a culture, then, I say, our chief occupation as artists, singly and jointly, should be the clarification of form, new alignments, in our own language and culture. . . .

I have maintained from the first that Eliot and Pound by virtue of their hypersensitivity (which is their greatness) were too quick to find a culture (the English continental) ready made for their assertions. They ran from something else, something cruder but, at the same time, newer, more dangerous but heavy with rewards for the sensibility that could reap them. They couldn't. Or didn't. But they both ended by avoiding not only the possibilities offered but, at the same time, the deeper implications intellectually which our nascent culture accented.

There is promise in Williams' American local, but—perhaps greater —there is an inherent responsibility to that local, that it be re-created in consonant, new forms. Notice, too, that he does not speak of the objects of a culture; he refers to the culture itself, an entity of great breadth and richness. As he had written early in *Paterson* V, "a place is made of memories as well as the world around it." For that reason, too, the poet Paterson is joyful as he *remembers*, the greatest of all human capabilities; and, as a result of his remembering, *returns* "to the old scenes/to witness/What has happened. . . ." In an earlier poem, "The Descent," Williams had affirmed,

> Memory is a kind
> of accomplishment,
> a sort of renewal
> even
> an initiation.

Life, culture, is more than the objective real. The giant Paterson has been dreaming throughout the epic; dreams, too, must be given credence. Later in *Paterson*, Williams describes Audubon who, in his Kentucky explorations, saw unicorn as well as buffalo. Even the most observant artist must be cognizant of the more-than-real, of "a secret world,/a sphere, a snake with its tail in/its mouth," symbolizing the impingement of the past—and the necessity for memory of it, as it "rolls backward into the past."

In 1950, Williams wrote (in a letter to Henry Wells) that there was a problem facing the artist, the problem to be both local and "at the same time to surmount that restriction by climbing to the universal." He aimed to do that by means of his poems, which he defined in the same letter:

> The poem to me (until I go broke) is an attempt, an experi-ment, a failing experiment, toward assertion with broken means but an assertion, always, of a new and total culture, the lifting of an environment to expression. Thus it is social, the poem is a so-

cial instrument—accepted or not accepted seems to be of no material importance. It embraces everything we are.

The poem (for I never if possible speak of poetry) is the assertion that we are alive as ourselves—as much of the environment as it can grasp: exactly as Hellas lived in the *Iliad*.

Necessary, then, is a knowledge of one's culture, one's local.
Those critics who feel that Williams' knowledge as he grew older
was narrow, prejudiced, or less than complete would do well to
refer to some of his later comments. In 1947, he speaks calmly of
existing "human greed and blindness"; in 1951, of the "tawdri-
ness" of the pervasive, "public" view of things. There is, however,
a simple and clear-sighted private view available to any perceptive man. It is this kind of realization that prompts him to write,
even when at his most depressed,

> A man wonders why he bothers to continue to write. And yet it is
> precisely then that to write is most imperative for us. That, if I can
> do it, will be the end of *Paterson,* Book IV. The ocean of savage
> lusts in which the wounded shark gnashes at his own tail is not
> our home.
>
> It is the seed that floats to shore, one word, one tiny, even micro-
> scopic word, is that which can alone save us.

Man is very much worth being salvaged. In "To Asphodel, That
Greeny Flower," Williams echoes and re-echoes this belief. That
salvation is possible is implied often in his use of the word *cure*.
Appearing frequently within *Paterson* and as the title of his last
play, the word recognizes illness. Yet, it is an affirmative designation: without a cure, there would be death. And a cure—for the
maladies of art as well as for those of man's spirit—does exist.

Williams offers no panaceas. He does not deny that the poem
must reflect life truly. He admits in a 1952 letter to John Holmes:

> What shall we say more of the verse that is to be left behind by
> the age we live in if it does not have some of the marks the age has
> made upon us, its poets? The traumas of today, God knows, are
> plain enough upon our minds. Then how shall our poems escape?
> They should be horrible things, those poems. To the classic muse
> their bodies should appear to be covered with sores. They should
> be hunchbacked, limping. And yet our poems must show how we
> have struggled with them to measure and control them. And we
> must SUCCEED even while we succumb. . . .

Enclosed with this particular letter, however, is Williams' "Triple Toast," the short, joyful verse in praise of a baby and the sexes that created it, "To give it place/In a stubborn world."

Throughout his career, Williams championed the creation of new life as one means of succeeding in the world, but he never forgot the necessity of artistic creation. In *I Wanted to Write a Poem*, he explained, "When you're through with sex, with ambition, what can an old man create? Art, of course, a piece of art that will go beyond him into the lives of young people, the people who haven't had time to create. The old man meets the young people and lives on." As Paterson the poet answers his own query in Book V, "What has happened to Paris/since that time?/and to myself?/ A WORLD OF ART/THAT THROUGH THE YEARS HAS/ SURVIVED!"

The world of art as it is mentioned in *Paterson* V refers first to Philippe Soupault's *The Last Nights of Paris*, the novel that Williams translated for publication in 1929. He admired the prose of the book, but more important to him was Soupault's concern with the mysterious Parisian whore—beautiful woman? good spirit? voice of the night? soul of Paris? In the ambiguity of this character may lie one prototype of Williams' later Paterson. At any rate, his mention of the novel early in the last book of the epic introduces one of the dominant themes of that section—ostensibly, the virgin-whore identity; more subtly, the virtue of selfless giving. And, on a wider base, the definition of *virtue* itself.

Critics who read *Paterson* V as a paean to art are overlooking this important cluster of themes. Admittedly, art to Williams is virtuous, as is the true artist. But so is the Portuguese mason who will not be content with inferior material, the English grandmother who loved well though unlawfully, all those of Williams' characters who have grace and pity, who will fight determinedly against "the age of shoddy." Virtue is doing one's best, despite human frailties. Virtue is also one critical means of judging the world—all segments of it.

Without question, virtue applies to art and the artist. Williams writes in *Paterson* V, "you cannot be/an artist/by mere ineptitude/The dream/is in pursuit!" Knowing one's craft is essential, but technical knowledge must be coupled with the dream, the "irrational," the heart. Virtue encompasses both sets of qualities. The wise men in Brueghel's painting of the Nativity are virtuous—as is Brueghel—because "they had eyes for visions/in those days."

So too is Joseph, husband of Mary, because he believed the words of the angel who appeared only in a dream. Were it not for Joseph's dream, who could have determined whether Mary was virgin or whore? The pattern occurs again in Williams' later writings. "The Farmers' Daughters," his last short story, has as its protagonist the "virtuous" whore Margaret. Similar characters are the housewife-nurse, the heroine of *The Cure*, and the Juarez whore in "The Desert Music." In an early version of the latter, Williams describes "The virgin of her mind." As he says firmly in *Paterson* V: "no woman is virtuous/who does not give herself to her lover/—forthwith."

Segments of these themes coalesce into one broad concern with virtue, and it is strange that readers have found here an unreasonable emphasis on art. What has been overlooked is that Williams is using his art objects as a means of recapitulating, of drawing together, earlier themes. Just as the *Last Nights of Paris* introduced such motifs as personal identity, the wasting on of time, the virgin-whore issue, the integrity of the artist, so Williams' reliance on the beautiful Flemish tapestry, "The Hunt of the Unicorn," serves to interrelate many themes which have appeared in all five books of *Paterson*. He does not didactically summarize what he has already said. Neither does he leave the poem to end with the concerns of Book V. Instead, he finds a concrete thing which embodies both the objects of the culture he loves and the personal qualities he has sought. Here is nature—birds and flowers in unimaginably vivid detail. Here is the young, mysteriously beautiful woman. Here is the greater-than-real Unicorn, his horn breaking into the high, white stars. And the creation of this masterpiece has been possible only because the artists were "All together, working together" according to a *design*.

The tapestry is important not only as the culmination of many separate themes but also as a way of perceiving Paterson the man. Williams seldom presents art objects in isolation. The tapestry, for example, appears as an integral part of Paterson's thoughts and experience, as in this passage:

> —every married man carries in his head
> > the beloved and sacred image
> > > of a virgin
> > whom he has whored
> > > but the living fiction
> > > > a tapestry

> silk and wool shot with silver threads
> a milk-white one-horned beast
> I, Paterson, the King-self . . .

Man's thoughts are a tapestry, a fiction: Paterson is in some ways the Unicorn, the King-self. Williams' juxtaposition of phrases, often without formal transition, is an effective method of re-creating the suddenness, the simultaneity, of human thought—in this case, of Paterson's thought.

Williams uses the same approach in his suite of poems on various of Brueghel's paintings. The poems attempt an accurate description of each painting, yet their weight is more often dependent on Williams' *non*-objective statement: "Brueghel the painter/concerned with it all"; "the mind the resourceful mind/ that governed the whole"; "The living quality of/the man's mind/ stands out." So involved is Williams with the character of the painter that the sequence might better be called "Pictures *of* Brueghel" rather than "Pictures from Brueghel."

To look upon Williams' interest in art as a symptom of his impatience with the concrete world seems even less defensible when one realizes that nearly every artist Williams admired is or was a devotee of the actual, the detailed depiction of life.

Then, too, it might well be considered that throughout his life Williams was deeply interested in the other arts. Few poets have been so willing to write introductions for plays (as well as plays themselves) or critiques for art exhibits. Having played the violin at one time, Williams felt that he had entrance also to the musical world. But it was to painting that he was most drawn, largely because of his great admiration for his mother's early work. Many of his closest friends were painters—Charles DeMuth, Charles Sheeler, Marsden Hartley. It seems reasonable, too, that the technical ferment in graphic art intrigued him as a possible parallel to the changes he was longing to see take place in poetry. For, throughout his career, he was deeply interested in the techniques of poetry. His criticism of an overt use of simile and a pretentious employment of symbolism is well-known. His respect for an enrichingly broad metaphor has become the basis for that figure's use in much contemporary poetry. But, of all the poetic concerns which could be labeled "technical," Williams was most involved with the problems of measure.

Emphatic as he was about the need for skill in poetry, it is increasingly to Williams' credit that he was seldom dogmatic about particular practices in themselves. He did not order a six-syllable line or a non-accentual verse pattern, although, as he wrote Richard Eberhart, he was insistent on the right measure ("musical pace"). He felt, however, that pace depended on an individual standard, one that could not be borrowed from another writer or "ordained" by an influential critic.

On two points, however, Williams *was* insistent: (1) that a measure of some kind was necessary, a means of giving the poem a regular movement; and (2) that the measure be flexible, or, in his scientifically oriented terms, "relative." From this stand eventually grew the variable or relative foot, arranged in the triadic line sequence of *The Desert Music* and *Journey to Love*. In 1953, he wrote of the triadic line that it was "an assembly of three-line groups arranged after a pattern which offers the artist, with much freedom of movement, a certain regularity." In 1955, he added that, "You cannot scan a line absolutely using a variable foot. Any one foot may consist of one syllable or even a cesura."

The 1955 poem "A Negro Woman" illustrates well the general symmetry of the triadic line, with several important variations. The opening lines include two one-syllable segments, the first—*wrapped*—set apart because of both pronunciation difficulty and its grammatical place in the sentence; the second—*bareheaded*—separated for pictorial emphasis.

> A Negro Woman
>
> carrying a bunch of marigolds
>   wrapped
>   in an old newspaper:
> She carries them upright,
>   bareheaded,
>   the bulk
> of her thighs
>   causing her to waddle
>   as she walks . . .

The leisurely, dignified pace is established. It is maintained throughout the short poem, lending strong emphasis to the metaphor which so surely places the woman in her proper, natural element:

> What is she
>   but an ambassador
>   from another world
> a world of pretty marigolds . . .

One is reminded of Williams' 1954 praise of Dylan Thomas' use of metaphor:

> he is outstanding in the way he packs the thought in among the words. For it is not all sound and image, but the ability to think is there also with a flaming conviction that clinches each point as the images mount. The clarity of his thought is not obscured by his images but rather emphasized ... it is the way the metaphors are identified with the meaning to emphasize it and to universalize and dignify it that is the proof of the poet's ability.

The conclusion of the poem, expressed in a simile, reinforces the effect of the stronger metaphor. The woman walks on; and one wonders whether, in her innocent pace, there is not more characterization than in the two figures of speech combined.

> ... a world of pretty marigolds
> of two shades
> which she announces
> not knowing what she does
> other
> than walk the streets
> holding the flowers upright
> as a torch
> so early in the morning.

Williams' practice is as effective audibly as it is visually. The three-line sequences give the impression of interweaving content, phrases independent yet closely related to the rest of the poem. Poems so arranged are usually wider than most of Williams' early poems, and the combination of space and print gives a leisurely effect. Audibly, such poems do move regularly: Williams' readings show that he gives each segment of line the same duration in time. One line may contain two syllables; the next, fifteen. The time value of each will be nearly the same, however, for various reasons of emphasis.

The most important principle about Williams' often-discussed triadic line is, I think, that he used it and defended it with no thought of forcing it on other poets. It seemed accurate for his work—at least, for some of it—and he used it when and where he could. He was, however, not afraid to contract the three-line sequences into the short tercets and quatrains of many of the brief poems in *Pictures from Brueghel*. He never forgot that every man must create his own measure. As he wrote in 1954 to Cid Corman,

What I want to emphasize is that I do not consider anything I have put down there as final. There will be other experiments but all will be directed toward the discovery of a new measure....

In a way, one could term Williams' very approach to technique "compassionate." Not only does he demand freedom for all poets to choose their own methods, but even his most satisfying theory of measure is flexible, dependent finally on the emotions of the poet or the poet-persona as he speaks within the poem. Such a tolerant attitude usually bespeaks confidence. As Williams wrote about René Char, the French poet he admired for numerous reasons:

> He is a man who adopts any form or no form at all with perfect indifference, writing regularly lines which scan perfectly or not according to the occasion, whatever it is. I envy and at the same time salute and love him.... The forms his verse take do not satisfy but then I understand how important to him is escape from any form at all; a man has to be well anchored to occupy that position.

That Williams, too, deserved to be called "well anchored" is perhaps difficult to prove conclusively in a short discussion. Surely, there are in his poems many echoes of what he described as his attitude of "long-range contentment," a contentment he achieved more or less despite his ready awareness of fact. As determined as he was to be heard in this world, it would indeed be grievous if readers could ignore his description of the poet as a man who "believes in his world, he believes in his people, and that's the reason he's a poet ... basic faith in the world." This is hardly the statement of a defeated man, or of a man likely to be defeated. Williams' later poems give definite proof that this is only the beginning for a spirit like his.

Sister Macaria Neussendorfer

William Carlos Williams' Idea of a City

To attempt an article on William Carlos Williams' "idea of a city" is to place oneself at once in the ambiguous position of being in danger of the medico-poet's own scorn. Continuously, vehemently, throughout his life he attacked those who would make the rational, the structured, and above all the imitative the most valid expression of life. He had a passion for the authentic as experienced here and now, and his own personal courage and vigor led him to explore and experience whatever aspects of life were open to him. This is not to say that he would have destroyed philosophy and literary criticism and government and institutional religion, but that he rebelled with a passion against the encroachment of such disciplines on the activity of the artist. For him, if art is not free it is nothing; free here meaning free from the tyranny of the rational within the artist as well as the traditional and structured —from whatever source—outside.

Already in 1945 he wrote in a letter to Norman Mcleod:

> When I say, and some well-meaning critic attacks my intelligence for saying it, that art has nothing to do with metaphysics— I am aiming at the very core of the whole matter. Art is some sort of an honest answer, the forms of art, the discovery of the new in art forms—but to mix that with metaphysics is the prime intellectual offense of my day. But who will understand that?
>
> The first part of *Paterson* begins my detailed reply.... The philosophers are trying to label the arts, to pigeonhole one's works without realizing that—they'll burn their fingers off in the end, if they are not careful—somewhere, in some piece of art resides a radioactive force beyond anything but their copying in their static spheres ... within [the artist] there burns a fiery light, too fiery for logical statement. It is not of the nature of logical statement.[1]

Reprinted from *Thought*, XL (Summer 1965), 242–72, by permission of *Thought*.
[1] William Carlos Williams, *Selected Letters of William Carlos Williams,* edited with an introduction by John C. Thirlwall (New York: McDowell, Obolensky, 1957), 238. Quoted by permission of Ivan Obolensky, Inc., New York.

The critic, then, is well warned that a search for system—for a narrow logical consistency—will be fruitless. The way is not closed, however, against attempting to understand. Meaning is there and perhaps, when finally understood, a meaning more ultimately valid than any facile product of surface-level celebration.

In an earlier letter (to James Laughlin in 1944) Williams made a remark which points to this deeper level: "I shan't quarrel with philosophy as such, let 'em have it. But there is a fallacy in always insisting that poetry shall 'mean' what some little stinker thinks it should. . . . What is sorely needed is poetic construction, ability in among the words, to invent there, to make, to make well and new." [2]

Words, as we well know, are the constructs not only of outward expression, but of that inner language by which we formulate to ourselves the meaning of experience, by which we translate into concept the multitudinous stimuli of present sensory perception, constantly relating them to memory and just as constantly readjusting remembered experience in the light of new associations. But the "radioactive force beyond" of which Williams speaks is not subject even to the tyranny of the inner word. It is free, indefinable, inexpressible (save in symbol). It is so close to the Self that the *I* cannot withdraw to properly scan it or make it logically comprehensible even to the mind emerging from it. It is an abyss, like the sea, of unfathomed depth, murky and treacherous, capable of lashing out into tempests fearful in their effects; and yet harboring treasures lovely beyond imagining.

But the poet must know the limitations of these inner powers. Williams was no advocate of automatic writing as substitute for poetic creation:

It's all right to give the subconscious play but not *carte blanche* to spill everything that comes out of it. We let it go to see what it will turn up, but everything it turns up isn't equally valuable and significant. That's why we have developed a conscious brain.

Of course the conscious writers, who know everything and must keep everything in perfect order—the ones I was railing against above—want us to believe that they *know*, that the church and its *intentions* are indispensable and right. They despise me. But I say and I believe that in despising me (microscopic as I am) they are in reality despising an essential part of the poetic process, the imaginative quota, the unbridled, mad—sound basis of all

---

[2] *Ibid.*, 219.

poems. They won't even consider me or what I intend. So be it. The academy must be served.

But isn't poetry, at its most significant, the antithesis of the academy? [3]

Smug formula, clear-cut morality, structured discipline of thought —nothing could be more stultifying to the teeming, kaleidoscopic creative centers of man. It is the agony and glory of the poet to be compelled to approximate the experience of this inner world in language. Language, which mysteriously was first formulated in the inner world to conceptualize outside reality, to make coin by which experience might be bartered, now must be wrenched to express inner experience to the outside world.

If there is any one characteristic than can be posited of experience, it is novelty. Williams was acutely conscious of this: "Now life is above all things else at any moment subversive of life as it was the moment before—always new, irregular. Verse to be alive must have infused into it something of the same order, some tincture of disestablishment, something in the nature of an impalpable revolution, an ethereal reversal, let me say." [4]

I. Language and the Local

Such a use of words—to express an order principled in nonorder —becomes an extremely complex problem when the tools of expression are in themselves traditional, communal, and relatively fixed. How can my word express *my* idea when the receiving mind will at once relate it to an experience that has been, and has been not mine but his? Such musing it undoubtedly was that led Williams to say, "I must object to the academic associations with which rhetoric is hung and which vitiate all its significance by making the piece of work to which it is applied a dry bone." [5]

Language, to be valid, must have its roots in the personal and the concrete. A poetry that floats on high shrouded in universals and tending to the cosmic proves, on closer reading, to be a mist of illusions. Such poetry has no validity; it cannot in truth speak to any man because it is not the voice of any man. It is a humbug. Williams felt very strongly that the American expatriate so common among his contemporaries was chasing a will-o'-the-wisp and

---

[3] *Ibid.,* 194.
[4] *Ibid.,* 23–24.
[5] *Ibid.,* 52.

he said so on more than one occasion to his friend Ezra Pound and to others about both Pound and Eliot. "There's no taboo effective against any land, and where I live is no more a 'province' than I make it. To hell with youse. I ain't tryin' to be an international figure. All I care about is to write." [6]

The place where he lived was for him cosmos enough, and he deplored the fact that too many American writers aspired to the international without the mediation of the local.

> Simply physical or external realism has an important place in America still. We know far less, racially, than we should about our localities and ourselves. But it is quite true that the photographic camera will not help us. We can, though, if we are able to *see* general relationships in local setting, set them down verbatim with a view to penetration. And there is a cleanliness about this method which if it be well handled makes a fascinating project in which every bit of subtlety and experience one is possessed of may be utilized. [7]

The local, then, is the natural field of experience. It is the home environment in which and through which one is most authentically in contact with reality. Here is an immediacy of response, a directness, and absence of self-conscious posturing which is simply not possible to a transplanted personality. Sameness and rootedness do not at all necessitate the dullness of routine or narrow obtuseness of spirit. Rather they prevent the inner sight from being blinded by the dust of novelty. They set the spirit free from the need to make gross adjustments and give it scope to exercise that subtlety which alone is able to reach to the heart of things. It was precisely this that Williams admired in Shakespeare: "His imagination kept him continually oscillating. . . . This is the sort of person who lives in one place, having no need to move his carcass in order to keep alive." [8]

Realization of the local is bound up with Williams' quest for adequate language. For him "form is never more than an extension of content" [9] but it *is* an extension, and therefore the two are inextricably united. Strictly speaking, of course, one could not say that

---

[6] *Ibid.,* 140.
[7] *Ibid.,* 146.
[8] William Carlos Williams, *Selected Essays of William Carlos Williams* (New York: Random House, 1954), 55.
[9] William Carlos Williams, *The Autobiography of William Carlos Williams* (New York: Random House, 1951), 330.

a word is what it says, but within the structure of a poem ("a structure built upon your own ground . . . your ground where you stand on your own feet" [10]) one can surely say that a word says what it does, that is, what it does to the receiver of the poem. And if the saying and the receiving are to be authentic, the word must be spoken from a context that is authentic by a person in the fullness of his being: "I won't follow causes. I can't. The reason is that it seems so much more important to me that I *am*." [11] How to find the language that will say to another what I am? Certainly not by crusading for causes or by turning to distant times or places. If there is a leading into universals, this comes after the fact. The important thing for the poet is to express the present reality. And he does this best by using the language that is naturally at hand:

> I have been watching speech in my own environment from which I expect to discover whatever of new is being reflected about the world. I have no interest as far as observation goes, in the cosmic. I have been actively at work (if such sketchy trials as I employ can be called such) in the flesh, watching how words match the act, especially how they come together. . . . All I want to do is to state that poetry, in its sources, body, spirit, in its form, in short, is related to poetry and not to socialism, communism or anything else that tries to swallow it; to reconcile this with the equally important fact that it deals with reality, the actuality of every day by virtue of its use of language. Doing so, naturally it reflects its time, by coincidence. . . . As I have said, for *me,* its virtue lies in relating to the immediacy of my life.[12]

This highly personal note is so marked in Williams' thinking as to be inseparable from any remembrance of his work. It is of a piece with his approach to reality: the most immediate object of experience is the Self. Where directness of experience is the mark of authenticity, it follows that the experiencing Self will be the center of attention. "The mind always tries to break out of confinement. It has tried every sort of interest which presents itself, even to a flight to the moon. But the only thing which will finally interest it must be its own intrinsic nature." [13]

---

[10] *Ibid.,* 376.
[11] Williams, *Letters,* 147.
[12] *Ibid.,* 129–131.
[13] *Ibid.,* 330–331.

To stop here would be to leave Williams open to a charge such as that made by Joseph Bennett: "As a poet Williams is intensely self-preoccupied, entranced with the image of his own ego. This preoccupation has its roots in his Romanticism, as does the concept of the self as the hero." [14] To the unjaundiced observer, however, it seems at least equally plausible that what prompts the self-preoccupation is not an immature egoism but a conviction that here is the foundation of all experienced reality: "possessors of knowledge in the flesh as opposed to a body of knowledge called science or philosophy." [15]

The habit of beginning *ab ovo* seemed connatural to Williams the physician who in a letter to Jean Starr Untermeyer, cloaking his thought in delightfully apt imagery, stated more specifically his reasons for emphasizing the beginnings of language within the self and the type of language which would spring natively from that self:

> Philosophy may and in fact must follow the poem. The poem is first.
>
> In short, I agree with everything you say, but I must insist that until the underlying mechanism is established you will never succeed in making it an organism. It must first be regrown from ground up—from the skeleton out *before* the flesh, the muscles, the brain can be put upon it. I am speaking from much further back or deeper down in the organization of the poem than you are. It may be my scientific training that enforces it, if so it is a good thing.
>
> It is amazing to me how the simple elements of the art are tacitly and erroneously assumed to be valid before they have been examined on their anatomic elements. Naturally, you can't blame most students for accepting the surely adventitious phenomenon of English prosody (in a new language where it doesn't apply and never has been applied) when all our language departments in our supposedly American universities are called English departments where English is taught and not our own tongue.[16]

The problem of finding (it is not a question of establishing or creating) an American prosody led to interesting and unusual experimentation in verse, and most strikingly in the long poem *Paterson*. The subject will be touched on once more in discussion of the poem itself.

---

[14]Joseph Bennett, "The Lyre and the Sledgehammer," *Hudson Review*, (Summer, 1952), 298.
[15] Williams, *Letters*, 137.
[16] *Ibid.*, 269.

II. The Idea of a City

Meanwhile, having sketched out, so to speak, the landscape of Williams' mind, we turn to the central topic, the idea of a city. That such a topic should have suggested itself for his most ambitious work is not surprising, for the city as symbol has had as long and varied a history, almost, as has the city as dwelling. Man's incurable habit of reflection has from time immemorial led him to see in the cities he has built—whether massive splendors of marble and gold and cedar in the ancient Orient or streamlined steel and concrete in modern America—a significance beyond the mere sum of dwelling places gathered for security and convenience. To some the city has meant glory, power, pleasure, excitement; for others it has signified darkness, toil, and the secret lure of evil. This dichotomy of view is evident also in the world of art and literature. Hopkins mourns the industrial barriers of smudge and smell erected by man against the grandeur of God's nature: "The soil is bare now, nor can foot feel, being shod," and Eliot finds the city dweller hollowed and frustrated in cosmopolitan ennui; while Dr. Johnson can declare categorically, "Whoever is tired of London is tired of life." Gertrude Stein sees Paris as the salvation of the artist, a place of freedom and creativity; Hardy sends his characters there for damnation.

In the world of myth and mystic, too, the city has its special significance. Here, however, vision seems more unified: the dwelling of the damned is seldom pictured as city; it is, rather, a place of shades, of darkness and isolation. It is for those who are saved to make their pilgrimages to the Sacred City on the Ganges or the Tiber or the Red Sea, and to find their ultimate fulfillment in that walled city of delights, the New Jerusalem.

Mystical insight and speculation, however, have no part in the idea of a city which Williams embodies in *Paterson*. "I know nothing of mysticism, Christian or otherwise," he once remarked in passing,[17] and—as has been said—the whole tenor of his work has been toward man as he is here and now. Interest in man is paramount in his myth of the city, for *Paterson* is about man; man identified with a city, the city personified. In the introductory note which gives a brief prose version of his insight, Williams explains:

---

[17] William Carlos Williams, "In Praise of Marriage," *Quarterly Review of Literature,* II (No. 2, 1944), 145.

This is . . . a long poem in four parts [now expanded to five] that
a man in himself is a city, beginning, seeking, achieving and concluding his life in ways which the various aspects of a city may
embody—if imaginatively conceived—any city, all the details of
which may be made to voice his most intimate convictions.[18]

This is, as Williams himself noted,[19] a metaphysical conception,
and one which encompasses both the poet's *Weltansicht* and his
idea of man. For it is "an interpenetration both ways": Mr. Paterson is Everyman (but presented in the only way we can directly
know him, as an individual—living in time, rooted in history), the
sum total of his experiences; he is also the city Paterson, which is
the cosmos in miniature, located in specified place ("only in some
one place does the universal ever become actual"). Williams is
consciously and deliberately distinguishing his concept from that
of those other writers of long poems in our time, Pound and Eliot.
Pound in *The Cantos* draws his inspiration from many cultures
and times: Provençal, Chinese, Italian, American; Eliot tends to
think more in terms of the universal, abstracting from place, for
"The place is always and only place and what is actual is actual . . .
only for one place." [20] To these views Williams once again took
vigorous objection:

> We live only in one place at a time but far from being bound by
> it, only through it do we realize freedom. Place then ceases to be
> a restriction . . . rather in that place, if we only make ourselves
> sufficiently aware of it, do we join with others in other places.
> [And furthermore] it is in the universal diversity of place that
> the actual gets its definition and vigor and that love itself is
> generated.[21]

The final statement points up again what little sympathy Williams had with those who associate art and beauty only with
European culture or with certain kinds of places, things or experiences. Life in all its wonderful diversity was source of poetic in-

---

[18] William Carlos Williams, *Paterson, Books I–IV,* "The New Classics
Series" (New York: New Directions, 1951), 7. (All later references will be
made to this edition.) Copyright 1946, 1948, 1949, 1951, © 1958 by William
Carlos Williams. Copyright © 1963 by Florence Williams. Reprinted by permission of New Directions Publishing Corporation.
[19] William Carlos Williams, *I Wanted to Write a Poem: The Autobiography
of the Works of a Poet,* ed. Edith Heal (Boston: Beacon Hill Press, 1958),
72.
[20] Thomas Stearns Eliot, "Ash Wednesday."
[21] William Carlos Williams, "A Fatal Blunder," *Quarterly Review of Literature,* II (No. 2, 1944), 125–126.

spiration to him, and no place or experience was to be counted too mean: "Locomotives," "Gay Wallpaper," "Burning the Christmas Greens." "I live where I live and acknowledge no lack of opportunity because of that to be alert to facts, to the music of events." [22] Having determined, then, to write of a city to express his concept of the city, it was inevitable that he should consider those with which he was familiar:

> What city?... New York? It couldn't be New York, not anything as big as a metropolis. Rutherford wasn't a city. Passaic wouldn't do. I'd known about Paterson, even written about it.[23] ... Suddenly it dawned on me that I had a find ... Paterson had a history, an important colonial history. It had, besides, a river— the Passaic, and the Falls. I may have been influenced by James Joyce who had made Dublin the hero of his book. I had been reading *Ulysses*. But I forgot about Joyce and fell in love with my city. The Falls were spectacular; the river was a symbol handed to me. I began to write the beginning, about the stream above the Falls. ... I took the river as it followed its course down to the sea; all I had to do was to follow it and I had a poem.[24]

"The poor who lived on the banks . . ."—always he comes back to the human. For him Paterson is both man and city, "a psychological-social panorama of a city treated as if it were a man," [25] both are at once concrete and universal, specified in time and place yet in symbol subsuming all time, all place, all men, all experience.

How unerring was the poet's instinct in choosing Paterson above other cities can best be experienced by a reading of the poem, but it is interesting to note how its geographic detail conforms to the *desiderata* listed by modern city planners. Kevin Lynch in *The Image of the City*, says, "Potentially, the city is in itself the powerful symbol of a complex society. If visually well set forth, it can also have strong expressive meaning. ... It may have strong structure or identity because of striking physical features [such as a great mountain, a river, or the sea] which suggest or impose their own pattern." [26]

---

[22] William Carlos Williams, a letter quoted in Janet Fiscalini, "Poet Americanus," *Commonweal,* LXX (September 18, 1959), 519–521.
[23] E.g., "For the Poem Paterson," *The Broken Span* quoted in *I Wanted to Write a Poem,* 68.
[24] William Carlos Williams, *I Wanted to Write a Poem,* 72–73.
[25] Williams, *Letters,* 216.
[26] Kevin Lynch, *The Image of the City* (Cambridge, Massachusetts: MIT and Harvard University Press, 1960), 5, 7.

Such a physical center of orientation is particularly desirable in view of man's tendency to organize his surroundings. It is part of the process of way-finding to form an environmental image as a kind of framework for existence, the image being a product of present perception and accumulated impressions from the past— economic, cultural, and political history gradually create a certain "character" for landmarks in a city, and it is well known that primitive races tend to erect their socially important myths around the framework of a striking landscape. For primitives as well as for many people today image tends to be hierarchical, so that there is a series of centers with gradations descending out to the peripheral. For the greater number of modern city-dwellers, however, the organization has a more dynamic understructure, partly because of the size of modern cities and partly because of the mobility of the inhabitants which results in constantly changing relationships between the subject forming the image and his environment. The complexity of the shifting relationship is well summarized in Lynch's opening paragraph:

> Like a piece of architecture, the city is a construction in space, but one of vast scale, a thing perceived only in the course of long spans of time. City design is therefore a temporal art, but it can rarely use the controlled and limited sequences of other temporal arts like music. On different occasions and for different people, the sequences are reversed, interrupted, abandoned, cut across. It is seen in all lights and all weathers.
>
> At every instant there is more than the eye can see, more than the ear can hear, a setting or a view waiting, to be explored. Nothing is experienced by itself, but always in relation to its surroundings, the sequence of events leading up to it, the memory of past experiences.[27]

One could hardly find, in the critical writings on the poem *Paterson*, a passage more aptly capturing its spirit or more definitively justifying the format into which Williams finally cast it. The process was, no doubt, partly intuitive ("The nascent instincts are the feelers into new territory." [28]), but there was also awareness of the labyrinthine intricacy of city and the difficulty of approximating this in poetry. What Williams said about the development of his poetic creed in general can apply here:

---

[27] *Ibid.,* 1.
[28] Williams, *Letters,* 252.

It wasn't at first much of an idea and didn't come like a burst of revelation. It was a gradual conviction that writing, and especially verse, has parts precisely as the human body has also of which it is made up and if a man is to know it, it behooves him to become familiar with those parts.

That took the whole field out of the realm of the emotions for their own sake and make it a study of means to an end.[29]

The end to be achieved in *Paterson* was the embodiment of the idea of a city in a poetic form which would incorporate the many and the one. Within the city the multiplicity of points of view, the ever new confrontation of relationships must be conveyed by both form and content. At the same time, for Williams the unity of the city was not merely architectural as it is for Lynch; it was organic.

And so the physical pattern of Paterson gave rise to its personification as a giant lying on his right side in a bend of the Passaic, his head near the thunder of the Falls, his back easily arched with the curve of the river. He lies ...

> Eternally asleep,
> his dreams walk about the city where he persists
> incognito. ...
> and the subtleties of his machinations
> drawing their substance from the noise of the pouring
> river
> animate a thousand automatons. Who because they
> neither know their own sources nor the sills of their
> disappointments walk outside their bodies aimlessly
> for the most part,
> locked and forgot in their desires—unroused.[30]

Here, at the outset, are stated some of those "most intimate convictions" of Williams' which the city embodies: its aspect of industrial center with concomitant economic problems, the closeness of nature and the determining influence of the natural phenomena which form and surround it, the unreal quality of the inhabitants who do not know their own identity because they are isolated by ignorance from their past; men who can neither respond to the creative impulses latent within them nor communicate with their fellows, locked in a terrible, sterile isolation. (The threat of isola-

---

[29] Williams, *Essays,* xiii.
[30] *Paterson,* 14. (Later references will be indicated in the text.)

tion had been upon the poet himself, and he revealed in a letter to Horace Gregory how consciously he strove to establish communion with the human family:

> Of mixed ancestry, I felt from earliest childhood that America was the only home I could ever possibly call my own. I felt that it was expressly founded for me, personally, and that it must be my first business in life to possess it; that only by making it my own from the beginning to my own day, in detail, should I ever have a basis for knowing where I stood. I must have a basis for orienting myself formally in the beliefs which activated me from day to day.[31])

III. Poetic Form

Disorientation, isolation, lack of personal identity—*Paterson* does indeed body forth the complex reality of modern man and his city, and it does so in what is perhaps the only form that could give adequate expression to such a milieu. Discarding the traditional logical, chronological or dramatic forms, it moves by way of associated images, themes, and symbols.[32] Its progression is somewhat like that of music: an idea is introduced in the guise of some image, is repeated over and over in varied forms, sometimes in a single line of melody, more often counterpointed by previously stated themes. As these are carried forward in their development, the first-stated theme may be dropped for a time only to recur unexpectedly and with grotesque or ironic effect in incongruous contexts. Much of our discussion here will be devoted to tracing these various themes, particularly as they are related to the poet's concept of the modern man-city. The whole scheme of movement—both in shifting rhythms of language and in hectic, helter-skelter confrontation of themes, views, persons, and events, both past and present—is wonderfully effective in capturing just that random sequence which would impinge on the composite consciousness of Paterson, the man-city. For a city seen from the abstract, from above, has design and ordered sequence. But as experienced by the man immersed in its bustle, it is not so. His view of the city is not governed by logic but by chance (when the light turns red he will turn

---

31 Williams, *Letters*, 185.
32 Gordon Kay Grigsby, "The Modern Poem: Studies in Thematic Form," *Dissertation Abstracts*, XXI, 622–23.

to notice a soft-eyed spaniel in the car alongside) and by the magnetism of association (they are putting a new front on the building where he first worked as office boy).

Of the formal composition of the poem, Williams was to say:

> In my mind all along, I was disturbed as to how I would put the thing down on the page. Finally I let form take care of itself; the colloquial language, my own language, set the pace. . . . I knew I had what I wanted to say. . . . I had to invent my form. . . . I was writing in a modern occidental world; I knew the rules of poetry. . . . I respected the rules but I decided I must define the traditional in terms of my own world.[33]

From this resolution came a unique collage effect gained by juxtaposition of documentary prose vignettes and poetic commentary or projection of related images. The relationship of the prose to the poetry achieves many times an almost startling effect by its seeming incongruity and many times a clear loveliness such as is found in his best imagistic pieces. In Book I, for example, there is a subtle progression from the poet's lament for the failure of language into the historic account of the mixed racial origins of "Jackson's Whites" and the Negroes of Barbados who speak with an Irish brogue. The selling of Irish women as slaves recalls the nine wives of an African Chieftain who, in a fine descriptive passage, are pictured in their unabashed primitive dedication to fertility. This in turn brings to mind the tragic death of a two-months bride, Mrs. Cumming, at the Passaic Falls. Her failure of communication with her young minister-husband as well as the "false language" of the newspaper account which sentimentalizes it, bring us back to a new poetic statement of the language theme. This interweaving of poetry and prose account is not always so successfully accomplished, particularly in the later books, but the author felt no obligation to apologize for this state of affairs. In a letter to Sister Bernetta Quinn concerning her perceptive study [34] of the poem Williams wrote:

> One fault in modern compositions . . . is that the irrational has no place. Yet in life (you show it by your tolerance of things

---

[33] Williams, *I Wanted to Write a Poem*, 73–74.
[34] Sister Bernetta Quinn, "William Carlos Williams; A Testament of Perpetual Change," *PMLA*, LXX (June, 1955), 292–322.

which you feel no loss at not understanding) there is much that
men exclude because they do not understand. The truly great
heart *includes* what it does not at once grasp, just as the great artist includes things which go beyond him. . . . The irrational enters
the poem in those letters, included in the text, which do not seem
to refer to anything in the "story" yet do belong somehow to the
poem—how, it is not easy to say.[35]

Concerning the use of prose and of seemingly prosaic details, Williams often and vehemently raised his voice in protest against the
use of the term "antipoetic" (coined by Wallace Stevens in his
preface to the 1934 *Collected Poems*): "The repeating of which
miscalculation makes me want to puke." [36] To him prose and verse
were the same thing, "both a matter of the words and an interrela-
tion between words for the purpose of . . . *the art*." And, as if to
claim authority for his "innovation," he says in Book Four:

> Sir Thopas (The Canterbury Pilgrims) says (to Chaucer)
>   Namoor—
>   Thy drasty rymyng is not
>   worth a toord
> —and Chaucer seemed to think so too for he stopped and went on
> in prose (p. 208).

Williams took pains to justify to his friends the longest piece of
prose, "the tail that would have like to wag the dog":

> The purpose of the long letter at the end [of Book Two] is
> partly ironic, partly 'writing' to make it plain that even poetry is
> writing and nothing else—so that there's a logical continuity in the
> art, prose, verse: an identity . . . The truth is there's an *identity*
> between prose and verse, not an antithesis . . . the long letter is
> definitely germane to the rest of the text—just as the notes follow-
> ing the *Waste Land* are related to the text of the poem. The differ-
> ence being that in this case the 'note' is subtly relevant to the
> matter and not merely a load for the mule's back. That it is *not*
> the same stuff as the poem but comes from below 14th St. is pre-
> cisely the key. It does not belong in the poem itself any more than
> a note on—Dante would.[37]

---

[35] Williams, *Letters,* 309.
[36] *Ibid.,* 263.
[37] *Ibid.,* 265.

To go into details of style beyond the question of the general form would take us outside the scope of this paper, but a few remarks on some stylistic devices which are particularly effective in echoing the characteristics of the milieu may be in order. For it is the *poetry* that matters: "No ideas but in things" echoes and re-echoes with growing insistence throughout the poem. His earlier apprenticeship in the school of Imagism had served him well—the concentration, the hard clear precision of the shifting pictorial detail conveys the thought with great effectiveness. And despite Williams' own fondness for the "descent" passage (Book Two, pp. 96–7—he mentions it in several letters and articles as the place where he began most surely to "find" his new prosody), it seems to the present writer that the philosophic overtones, so reminiscent of the *Four Quartets*, the lack of definite detail and the use of connectives lengthening the unit of thought make this section almost foreign to *Paterson*—if "foreign" can be used in connection with anything appearing in that poem. The sure touch appears rather in such passages as these:

> Three middle aged men with iron smiles
> stand behind the benches—backing (watching)
> the kids, the kids and several women—and
> holding,
>   a cornet, clarinet, and trombone,
> severally, in their hands, at rest.
>   There is also,
> played by a woman, a portable organ . . (p. 80)
>   The sun
> winding the yellow bindweed about a
> bush; worms and gnats, life under a stone.
> The pitiful snake with its mosaic skin
> and frantic tongue. The horse, the bull
> the whole din of fracturing thought
> as it falls tinnily to nothing upon the streets
> and the absurd dignity of a locomotive
> hauling freight—(p. 34)

The diction attuned to everyday speech, with the most simple and direct substantives modified by sparse but telling descriptive words—"iron smiles," "mosaic skin," "frantic tongue,"—the concern with individual persons—"middle aged men"—and things; all these are typical and serve subtly to underscore his view of the man-city: the universal through the local.

IV. Imagery and Symbol

Of traditional imagery, especially simile, there is little evidence; indeed, it would be surprising if the case were the contrary, for in Williams' existential city what could be said to be like something else? Rather there are the multitudinous subtle metaphors and symbols compounded to convey the complexity of modern man in his quest for self-realization. The poet once wrote to Oswald LeWinter, "An artist should always speak in symbols even when he speaks most passionately; otherwise his vision becomes blurred. He has to hold his objects away from him to be able to see them clearly." [38] In such a way he uses dogs, for example: lame dogs, washed dogs, unleashed dogs, dogs who insist on mating even against man's "Nay" and in the final book, tapestried dogs in the yelping excitement of the hunt. Sometimes they are symbol of the poet (as in the Preface "Sniffing the trees,/just another dog/ among a lot of dogs"; but he is a lame dog who digs a musty bone while his fellows in happy oblivion run after rabbits), sometimes they are symbol of his thought dashing in and out among life's experiences, and sometimes they are there for pure "dogginess": a protest against urban man's divorce from nature.

Occasionally there is an irresistible, arbitrary surrealistic image like the one which epitomizes the whole concept of the feminine principle in Book One:

> . . Womanlike, a vague smile,
> unattached, floating like a pigeon
> after a long flight to his cote (p. 23).

The surrealistic technique is operative also in the "perpetual change" which has been so well pointed up by Sister Bernetta. Mr. Paterson's thoughts (p. 18) sit and stand inside the bus, alight, scatter, suddenly fuse into plateglass, and then are listed in the Telephone Directory—delightfully like the chain of responses a half-conscious modern mind might make on its way to work in the morning. One can hardly imagine the primitive or even medieval man so experiencing reality, for the series of events by which they were surrounded was limited, so that when attention was not withdrawn from external events, it was likely that one could be aware

---

[38] *Ibid.,* 319.

of what was going on. For Paterson it is patently impossible to
advert to all the stimuli of sight and sound and smell and personal
presences, and so his thoughts are semi-awarenesses and fluid associations melting into one another. The African proto-wife, too, is
metamorphosed—changed into the log she straddles while her suc-
cessors become branches springing from her thighs, as deep-seated
archetypes of fertility rise up from the inner wells of the poet's
consciousness. Roots of trees writhe on the ground, and the poet
himself becomes Daphne (with a difference!):

> His ears are toadstools, his fingers have
> begun to sprout leaves (his voice is drowned
> under the falls) (p. 102).

Such images with their shifting dream-like quality serve in their
various contexts to reinforce the feelings of insecurity, uncertainty,
isolation, frustration, and lack of self-knowledge which Paterson experiences. They are symptomatic on the psychological level in exact
correspondence to violence and violation on the physical level—
themes which likewise recur throughout. But they also—in spite of
themselves, so to speak—testify to the soundness of that deeper
self-knowledge which resides below the level of conscious thought.
At this level they ring true, and by that very fact give expression
to the surface tensions.

A further quality of style operates very markedly to reveal Williams' concept: the kinetic power of his verbs.

> Jostled as are the waters approaching
> the brink, his thoughts
> interlace, repel and cut under,
> rise rock-thwarted and turn aside
> but forever strain forward—or strike
> an eddy and whirl, marked by a
> leaf or curdy spume, seeming
> to forget   .
> Retake later the advance and
> are replaced by succeeding hordes
> pushing forward—they coalesce now
> glass-smooth with their swiftness,
> quiet or seem to quiet as at the close
> they leap to the conclusion and
> fall, fall in air!   (p. 16)

The movement of the water here caught in all its tumultuous activity just before the dizzying plunge is apt figure for the present moment of time in Paterson's teeming thoughts and the multifarious life of the city—the ruthless, restless, endless activity of a city in the Western world.

The forcefulness and the almost brusque directness of phrase likewise give expression to the thought and attitude of Williams himself: his affirmation of life, his virile appetite for knowledge and conquest, his active and startling habit of challenge.

> Smash the world, wide!
> —if I could do it for you—
> Smash the wide world.
> a fetid womb, a sump!   (p. 201)

And yet there are the letters from the woman-poet "C" and from "T.J." presupposing his compassion, and quiet lyric interludes where questions are lost in ecstatic peace:

> We sit and talk,
> quietly, with long lapses of silence
> and I am aware of the stream
> that has no language, coursing
> beneath the quiet heaven of
> your eyes   (p. 35)

V. Man-City

We come, then, to a further elaboration of the city-idea: it is not only Paterson, New Jersey, and the fictive Mr. Paterson, poet and sometime doctor. Like

> Uranium, the complex atom, breaking
> down, a city in itself, that complex
> atom, always breaking down   (p. 209)

the experiencing subject of *Paterson* can be broken down to its final unit: the individual existing man, Dr. Williams himself. But far from finding this a barrier to the effectiveness of the poem as have Joseph Bennett, who objects to Williams' "self-pre-occupation," or Edwin Honig, who feels that the role of poet-as-city is so specialized as to limit seriously the universal relevance,[39] we can see in it the

---

[39] Edwin Honig, "The *Paterson* Impasse," *Poetry,* LXXIV (April, 1949), 39.

final application of his own dictum: No experiences but in and through persons.

But the situation also gives rise to inevitable tensions: as conscious, experiencing being, Williams is dedicated to the real, to a safeguarding the integrity of things, to an acceptance of life in its fullness. As poet he is "dedicated to the word, the verbal invention, the poetic expression." [40]

> The vague accuracies of events dancing two
> and two with language which they
> forever surpass—   (p. 34)

"Rigor of beauty is the quest," he says in the Preface (p. 11), "But how will you find beauty when it is locked in the mind past all remonstrance?" The refinement of meaning evident in choice of a word such as "remonstrance" is in itself partial answer to the question, for adequate language is the poet's way of unlocking the treasures of beauty.

However, he realizes that in the very act of consigning his thought to language, albeit expressive language, he condemns it to a kind of mummified death:

>   And there,
>   in the tobacco hush: in a tepee they lie
>   huddled (a huddle of books)
>   antagonistic,
>   and dream of
>   gentleness—under the malignity of the hush
>   they cannot penetrate and cannot waken, to be again
>   active but remain—books
>   that is, men in hell,
>   their reign over the living clearly ended   (p. 140)

With sudden intensity the agony of the paradox takes hold of him. (The verbal echoes of "clearly! Clearly?" which elsewhere re-create birdsong in the forest, here take on a bitter irony.)

> Clearly, they say. Oh clearly! Clearly?
> What more clear than that of all things
> nothing is so unclear, between man and
> his writing, as to which is the man and
> which the thing and of them both which
> is more to be valued   (p. 140)

---

[40] *Ibid.,* 38.

Throughout Book Three the burning of the library engenders a
sense of tragedy and a yearning ("Beautiful thing . . . beautiful
thing . . . beautiful thing! aflame") for what has been lost. Books
are a refuge from the overpowering vitality of the present:

> Books will give rest sometimes against
> the uproar of water falling   (p. 119)

Or provide shelter against the sun of naked being which beats
upon the mind exposed always to reality:

> A cool of books
> will sometimes lead the mind to libraries
> of a hot afternoon, if books can be found
> cool to the sense to lead the mind away.   (p. 118)

But there is an intense consciousness that this is a cool wind, "a
ghost of a wind" which leads the mind astray. We are all too apt to
confuse "which is the wind and/which the wind's power over us/to
lead the mind away." And so the realist in Williams breaks out in
angry rebellion against the maker of books, condemning

> a nothing, surrounded by
> a surface, an inverted
> bell resounding, a
>
> white-hot man become
> a book   (p. 149)

VI. Divorce

As the search for the real and the significant continue, there is
borne in on him the agonized consciousness of divorce and the
incessant need for communication, both within himself and with
others, which form the major theme of *Paterson:*

> Divorce is
> the sign of knowledge in our time,
> divorce! divorce!   (p. 28)

This cry is ringingly repeated like the prophet's voice calling out in
the streets. ("There are always at least two poets in William Carlos
Williams," observes Honig, "the exquisite miniaturist and the be-

sieged expositor of human values." [41]) But deep as the longing is for wholeness, he seems to see a value in life's duality also: "Embrace the foulness/—the being taut, balanced between eternities," he advises himself when contemplating Harry Leslie crossing the Falls on a tightrope (p. 26). And in celebrating the discovery of radium by "Curie: woman (of no importance) genius" he becomes even more explicit in his recognition of the creative energies latent in a dialectical system:

Dissonance
(if you are interested)
leads to discovery   (p. 207)
Love, the sledge that smashes the atom?
No, No! antagonistic cooperation is the key, says Levy.   (p. 208)

Such a process of reducing the multiple, at least temporarily, to one; or, to put it another way, to develop the kind of vision that sees beyond the heterogeneous outer elements into the inner dynamo of power which activates them—this is precisely the task and intention of a poem whose subject is a man-city:

.   .   a mass of detail
to interrelate on a new ground, difficultly;
an assonance, a homologue
triple piled
pulling the disparate together to clarify
and compress.   (p. 30)

But divorce is understood too as the separation which leaves man sterile and isolate. This tragedy strikes on many levels—domestic, intellectual, economic, artistic. Recalling the death plunge of young Mrs. Cumming into the Falls, Williams recaptures the scene in the configuration of the text and tries to fathom the depths of her secret misery:

She was married with empty words:
better to
stumble at
the edge
to fall
fall

---

[41] *Ibid.,* 39.

                                        and be
                                        —divorced
        from the insistence of place—
                                        from knowledge,
        from learning—the terms
        foreign, conveying no immediacy, pouring down.
                                        —divorced
        from time (no invention more), bald as an
        egg   .
                and leaped (or fell) without a
        language, tongue-tied
                        the language worn out   .   (pp. 102–3)

The failure of communication is the prime concomitant of divorce, whether considered under the aspect of language or of sexual
intercourse. The Passaic River is early introduced as symbol of the
former; it is at once the stream of Paterson's thought and the language by which that thought is communicated:

            (What common language to unravel?
            .   .   combed into straight lines
            from that rafter of a rock's
            lip.)   (p. 15)

Its very history and geology and geographic pattern make the river
expressive of incomplete communication, George Zabriskie informs
us, for it is a postglacial river which, having been blocked in its
passage, now curves in devious ways through a more shallow bed.[42]
    The pathos and unashamed anguish of citizens who fail to de-
velop a common language is expressed in a number of ways, but
chiefly through the series of excerpts from a lonely girl's letters.
She is completely self-aware—too much so, perhaps—and tells
Paterson, who has rejected her confidences, that her inner life has
in consequence taken on an unreality and inaccessibility which
make any creative work impossible. Sam Patch, too, was a victim
of the failure of language: after his last speech at the Genesee
Falls he inexplicably faltered in his dive and hurtled to his death.
When his body was found frozen in ice the next March Paterson
saw yet another symbol of its own isolation and coldness.

---

[42] George Zabriskie, "The Geography of Paterson" *Perspective,* VI (Au-
tumn-Winter, 1953), 212.

The terrifying implications of failure to communicate are inversely expressed in a vividly picturesque passage near the close of Book One:

> Thought clambers up,
> snail like, upon the wet rocks
> hidden from sun and sight—
>   hedged in by pouring torrent—
> and has its birth and death there
> in that moist chamber, shut from
> the world—and unknown to the world,
> cloaks itself in mystery—
>   And the myth
> that holds up the rock,
> that holds up the water thrives there—
> in that cavern, that profound cleft,
>   a flickering green
> inspiring terror, watching   .   .
> And standing, shrouded there, in that din,
> Earth, the chatterer, father of all
> speech . . . .   (pp. 51–2)

The cavern with its pouring torrent flickering green among rocks where thought clambers up is a wonderfully wrought symbol of the subsconscious, from which thought, in a sense, has its birth and death. There is a din of water thriving—these powers cloaked in mystery are never at rest. Thought clambers up snail like, for conscious formulation of thought requires effort and seems slow and labored by contrast with the spontaneous creative forces. But climb it must, to give outward expression to what must else remain unknown to the world, and in its death would slip back on the wet rocks to become poison-breeding decay in the sea from whence it came. If the imaginative and intuitive powers are as hidden waters, the faculty of speech is earth; what it lacks in fluidity and effortless adaptability, it gains in solid permanence and exterior perceptibility. It is Earth who is father of all speech. The healthy natural man is natively, by heritage, able to chatter—to communicate without artificial blockage. Failure to find a language is symptomatic, then, not only of a cleavage between man and man, but between man and father Earth—that final uprooting which sets man adrift in complete ineffectuality.

Coupled with failure to find a meeting of minds is the terrible failure to communicate wholly and healthily even on the physical level. *Paterson* teems with recordings of this type of failure, and it seems to be in Williams' view a basic evil in our society; one of which he, in his capacity as physician, would be acutely conscious. Fertility of body and creativity of mind are to him correlative in some way. "Convention or habit is a tyrannous master; all decency (and that's what makes men rebels) enforces it. Sex is one lead out of our dilemma, and that is why many men take it. That sex is intimately concerned with the rebellious mind is of significance, and that few men see its significance leads us to most of the torments of our early youth." [43]

In Book Five he considers the "Nativity" by Peter Brueghel the Elder with joyous approbation, but adds,

> no woman is virtuous
> who does not give herself to her lover
> —forthwith.

The virgin and the whore seem to him "an identity"—seeing, perhaps, in a purely arbitrary denial, pride of power and will to humiliate, as much of abuse as in promiscuous indulgence for the sake of gain. "In too much refinement there lurks a sterility that wishes to pass too often for purity when it is anything but that." [44] His affirmation is always on the side of healthy fulfillment:

> "Loose your love to flow"
> while you are yet young
> male and female.

Here even more than elsewhere Williams is conscious of the duality of life, and he proclaims it with vigor and healthy joy. Already in *In the American Grain* he had expressed his admiration for the Jesuit Père Rasles in his work with the Indians (it is significant that D. H. Lawrence reviewed this book and liked it):

His sensitive mind. For everything his fine sense, blossoming, thriving, opening, reviving—not shutting out—was tuned ... It is *this* to be *moral*: to be *positive*, to be peculiar, to be sure, generous, brave—TO MARRY, to *touch*—to *give* because one HAS, not because one has nothing.[45]

---

[43] Williams, *Letters,* 329.
[44] *Ibid.,* 155.
[45] William Carlos Williams, *In the American Grain* (New York: New Directions Paperbook, 1956), 121.

The same almost boundless affirmation is brought to bear on the polarity of sexes throughout *Paterson* and with it the bitter disillusion of frequent failure in love. At the very opening, no sooner is the man-city introduced than Garrett Mountain is personified *das ewig Weibliche* asleep in his arms. Symbols are multiplied: the river is "the multiple seed," the juniper tree becomes a phallus; sex attraction is "thick lightnings that stab at the mystery of man," and, with the breadth of his experience as doctor and man, he calls it also " a sleep, a source, a scourge." One of the loveliest and most authentic symbols of sexual union is the stream itself. It begins quite explicitly yet does not oversimplify because the mystery touches deeply not only on communication, but on the sense of reality which is bound up in time and in being itself:

> I wish to be with you abed, we two
> as if the bed were the bed of a stream
> —I have much to say to you
>   ... to
> go to bed with you, to pass beyond
> the moment of meeting, while the
> currents float still in mid-air, to
> fall—
> with you from the brink, before
> the crash—
>   to seize the moment.   (p. 35)

There is established thus early in the poem the link between language and sex—each is a way of knowing the Other (as the scriptural use of "know" so beautifully implies); each can be a deep enrichment of the Self, yet each is subject to abuse by frivolous staying on the surface. "I have much to say to you"—in Paterson the question is: Will I be able to say it? And will you be able to receive truly the Self that I offer?

"As if it were the bed of a stream." The rushing water is so apt a symbol of the experience that it is in the nature of an archetype, one closely linked with death; as the lover loses his identity in the Other, the waters momentarily close over him and "The moment of meeting" becomes timeless: "the currents float still in mid-air" as the two are now not only individuals but representatives of a race, poised above the flow of time by virtue of the mystery which lifts them out of themselves. But the river comes to the Falls, and even as time is transcended it comes to claim its own in the crash down over the rocks into the dizzying swirls and eddies below. Sex, like language, is limited. It is an attempt to reach out to the infinite, to break the circle of limited reality, but it is doomed to come full cycle in the return to Self.

The same sequence of thought is found again in Book Five in more compressed form:

> a secret world,
> a sphere, a snake with its tail in
> its mouth
> > rolls backward into the past

Here the sexual is subordinated to the symbolism of time and timelessness, yet the snake at once suggests the sexual. An additional association follows on this, as serpent recalls to mind the Eden of primeval days when sex was not "a secret world" and also the Egyptian Isis and all that is implied of sex as solemn ritual, both ecstasy and act of worship.

After a very frank prose interlude describing an encounter with a whore, the serpent returns in another guise:

> A lady with the tail of her dress
> on her arm.

And so we are brought back to the role of woman, which is explored early in Book One. Paterson's woman-mountain also undergoes a metamorphosis:

> a man like a city and a woman like a flower
> —who are in love. Two women. Three women.
> Innumerable women, each like a flower.
> > But
> only one man—like a city.   (p. 15)

Woman is multiple: wife, mother, nurse, companion; yet never achieves all in an ideal way. So there are innumerable women, and man's search for satisfaction, for the complete perfect union is unending. The freshness of flower beauty does not long remain to the women, however, "the tongue of the bee/ misses them/ They sink back into the loam . . . shiver as they wilt and disappear:/ Marriage come to have a shuddering implication/" (p. 20). Sterility and fear of fertility abound, from the housewife's letter about Musty (p. 69) to the long Lesbian passage opening Book Four.

> Sing me a song to make death tolerable, a song
> of a man and a woman: the riddle of a man
> and a woman.   (p. 131)

Death—it is inevitable that thoughts of birth and copulation should also lead to death:

> For what is there but love, that stares death
> in the eye, love, begetting marriage—
> not infancy, not death.   (p. 130)

Death, like love, appears in twofold aspect, but here the negative note of violence and destruction is given emphasis. Rarely is there such peace as in, "Death lies in wait,/ a kindly brother . . . The radiant gist that resists the final crystallization" (p. 133). The history of the land is filled with accounts of violent deaths: a father murders his six-month-old baby Nancy and buries her in a paper sack under a rock (p. 229); John Johnson kills an old Dutch couple for money (and doesn't get any) and is himself hanged on Garrett Mountain; the *Gesangverein* is dispersed by a maniac's pistol when they trample down his lawn. Earlier still (p. 125) the gentle Delaware Indians were stung to violence by the brutality of the white man whose bestiality was an offense to the savage.

> Do you still believe—in this
> swill-hole of corrupt cities?
> Do you, Doctor, Now?   (p. 132)

"Rigor of beauty is the quest," and in this nine months' wonder rolling up out of chaos: the city, there is also beauty side by side with the waste farina in the sink and lumps of rancid meat. Where to find beauty? Paterson rejects the solution of the populace ("that great beast" Hamilton called them) who come to the Park for pleasure.

> It is all for
> pleasure . their feet . aimlessly
> wandering.   (p. 70)

And they leave the woman-mountain ravaged and torn. He, too, comes to the park: "Outside/ outside myself/ there is a world,/ he rumbled, subject to my incursions—a world (to me) at rest,/ which I approach/ concretely—." So he walks through the park and finds nature's answer to his quest for beauty: the antlered sumac, the churring flight of the partridge, the chipmunk scampering with tail erect, and in the background the roar of the river and the sun-stained tapestry of the Falls. But the idyll is marred by the intrusion of drunken, impotent lovers and the distant harangue of an Evangelist "jumping up and down in his ecstacy." He preaches about the beauty of poverty to the patient poor, the children, who have nothing to renounce. In planning this section, Williams had indicated his topic would be "the economic distress occasioned by human greed and blindness—aided, as always, by the church, all churches in the broadest sense of that designation—." [46]

VII. The Artist and His World

Paterson reflects on Federal Reserve System and Hamilton's one-time grandiose schemes for establishing a national power center at the Falls (two hundred and forty-seven undershot water wheels actually were in operation at one time)—a train of thought which returns to him over and over, until in Book Four and Five he devotes whole pages to the explanation of National Credit vs. Usura (Federal Reserve). Williams rather amusingly made known his source for these ideas (as if he had to!) by adopting Pound's own shorthand and speech idiom. Or was it intended to be amusing? In any case, Paterson turns from the preacher with the same gnawing question:

> Is this the only beauty here?
> And is this beauty—
> torn to shreds by the
> lurking schismatists?   (p. 88)

But he grants a margin of doubt in favor of the zealous Klaus Ehrens:

> Unless it is beauty
> to be, anywhere,
> so flagrant in desire.   (p. 88)

Williams admired in any man a whole-hearted dedication, and so agreed this may be "the beauty of holiness." But with the

---

[46] Williams, *Letters,* 301.

preacher's doctrine he had little patience and the whole scene is so constructed as to be always bordering on the satiric. The pentecostal enthusiasm of the preacher is canceled out by the prearranged response "Amen! Amen!" of the "devout assistants" and their use of brass instruments to capture an audience and whip it up to fervor. To counteract such transcendental attitudes, Paterson adopts a completely opposite creed, underscoring the immanent:

> You also, I am sure, have read
> Frazer's Golden Bough. It does you
> Justice—a prayer such as might be made
> by a lover who
> appraises every feature of his bride's
> comeliness and terror—
> terror to him such as one, a man
> married, feels toward his bride—
>
> . . .
>
> The Himalayas and prairies
> of your features amaze and delight—
>
> . . .
>
> The world spreads
> for me like a flower opening—and
> will close for me as might a rose—
>
> wither and fall to the ground
> and rot and be drawn up
> into flower again. But you
> never wither—but blossom
> all about me. In that I forget
> myself perpetually—in your
> composition and decomposition
> I find my . .
>   despair! (pp. 92–3)

Like much else in the poem, this is an exploration of the possibilities. The cyclic view of life is found—as is inevitable—to lead to fatalistic despair. That Williams had a deep distrust of the formalized, the oversimplified and the unrealistic in religion comes as no surprise. In regard to symbolism he wrote to Kenneth Burke: "You know the dead-serious sort who know nothing of the symbolic. Or is there such a sort which does not postpone its heaven to another world—the deadliest symbol of all?" [47] What seems to

---

[47] *Ibid.*, 257.

trouble most of all is that there should be any sham—typical of
this was a chance comment: "Plot is like God: the less we formulate it the closer we are to the truth." [48]

The quest for beauty—"Beautiful thing"—continues throughout
Book Three where Paterson's past is explored, particularly the dis-
asters by fire, flood and tornado which ravaged the city in 1920.

> Beautiful thing:
> —a dark flame,
> a wind, a flood—counter to all staleness.   (p. 123)

seems to be an answer to an earlier sigh:

> Why have I not
> but for imagined beauty where there is none
> or none available, long since
> put myself deliberately in the way of death?
> Stale as a whale's breath: breath!
> Breath!

The variousness of the world seems for a time to stave off the sense
of staleness. But it returns, and the Library is consigned to flames
because it has "not one volume of distinction." The world of the
university is scorned at once and continuously as solving nothing.
In this city there are "no ideas but in things," and Williams clears
himself of the role of academician in a novel contrast:

> Certainly I am not a robin nor erudite,
> no Erasmus nor bird that returns to the same
> ground year by year.   (p. 29)

But his strongest indictment comes when he seeks into the reasons
why knowledge is restricted ("knowledge undispersed, its own un-
doing" he has said in the Preface):

> Who restricts knowledge?
>   ... And if it is not
> the knowledgeable idiots, the university,
> they at least are the non-purveyors
> should be devising means
> to leap the gap.   (p. 46)

---

[48] *Ibid.,* 146.

He lays a heavy responsibility at the feet of the academy, then, to contribute to the reintegration of life; however, he does not look there for inspiration or contact with the real or for beauty, but only

> that the poet
> in disgrace, should borrow from erudition (to
> unslave the mind). (p. 99)

The artist has other quarrels; with the unlearned as well as with the learned, and Paterson is acutely conscious of his isolation. He is the lame dog. He is the dwarf of ill proportion who refrains from being active on either side (p. 19), an object of idle interest to his fellow men, yet lacking in genuine communion with them.

> The dwarf lived there, close to the waterfall—
> saved by his protective coloring.
> Go home. Write. Compose .
> Ha!
> Be reconciled, poet, with your world, it is
> the only truth!
> Ha! (p. 103)

So he taunts himself, and so do men taunt him. "I have said that the artist is an Ishmael; call me Ishmael says Melville in the very first line of Moby Dick; he is the wild ass of a man—Ishmael means affliction." So Paterson's correspondent sums up the situation (p. 40). Paterson must try, however, to keep in touch with the world of reality, for it is the source of his creative activity: "Outside/ Outside myself/ there is a world subject to my incursions." When he visits the Park, he must do it walking: "The body is tilted slightly forward . . . and the weight thrown on the ball of the foot . . ."—so far is he separated from the ordinary in life that he must review a basic exercise book to recall the motions! But he does not become so involved in activity as to lose his function as artist. When asked what he is doing he replies:

> "What do I do? I listen to the water falling. (No
> sound of it here but with the wind!) This is my entire
> occupation." (p. 60)

His position as seer does not go unchallenged, however, and he becomes the victim of jealous rage:

in the air, slow, a crow zigzags
with heavy wings before the wasp-thrusts
of smaller birds circling about him
that dive from above stabbing for his eyes.   (p. 61)

And even his friends fail to comprehend either his message or his
inner need to voice it as he can:

Give up
the poem. Give up the shilly-
shally of art.   (p. 132)

Or, Geez, Doc, I guess it's all right
but what the hell does it mean?   (p. 138)

For the artist more than for any other, it is necessary to find a language to reopen communication with his world. But it must be his
own world that provides inspiration and it must be his native language that expresses it

warn you, the sea is *not* our home.
the sea is not our home.
I say to you, Put wax rather in your
ears against the hungry sea
it is not our home!   (p. 235)

The final striking portrait of Paterson in Book IV shows him re-
turning from the sea (the world at large) whither the river had
carried him, eating the fruit of his own country and heading inland with his faithful dog—turning his back on foreign lands to be
an American poet.

VIII.   Art As Fulfillment

Concerning the more recently published Book V,[49] Williams said:

Paterson V must be written, is being written . . . Why must it be
written? *Paterson IV* ends with the protagonist breaking through
the bushes, identifying himself with the land, with America. He
finally will die but it can't be categorically stated that death ends

---

49 William Carlos Williams, *Paterson, Book V* (New York: New Directions,
1958). Quoted by permission of New Directions, New York.

anything. When you're through with sex, with ambition, what can an old man create? Art, of course, a piece of art that will go beyond him into the lives of young people, the people who haven't time to create. The old man meets the young people and lives on.[50]

This is his final answer to the question of beauty's permanence: "A WORLD OF ART? THAT THROUGH THE YEARS HAS SURVIVED!" His dominant image throughout the book is taken from the Unicorn tapestries in "The Cloisters." Louis Martz [51] has with fine perception pointed out the happy correspondence between "The Hunt of a Unicorn" and *Paterson.* The tapestries achieve their success through combination of the local and the mythical. In the background are one hundred and one shrubs, trees, and herbs so perfectly woven that eighty-five of them have been identified by botanists. The whole is constructed with a free disregard of perspective and with intermingled brutal faces of varlets and hounds. The analogy is so obvious as not to need comment.

A milk-white one horned beast
I, Paterson, the King-self

Paterson, the poet thus becomes identified with the unicorn, incarnate spirit of Art, to live on in the minds of men.

And lest it be objected that the poet has in this final word betrayed his original purpose of being true to the realm of things-as-they-are, we observe that it had not been defined what things are, but only that they are. There has been no change in the method of approach; the creative force generated by dialectic opposition is still recognized—his medical experience of the "violent antithesis of death and decay, over against reproduction and renewal" conditioned Williams' mind so that he could write, "After thirty years of staring at one true phrase he discovered that its opposite also was true." [52] The imagination is still the power which functions in opposing art to the unhappy fact of decay. Ezra Pound in an essay on Williams reconciled with great acuity the natural vigor of the man with the idealism of the poet:

---

[50] Williams, *I Wanted to Write a Poem,* 22.
[51] Louis Martz. "The Unicorn in *Paterson:* William Carlos Williams," THOUGHT, XXXV (Winter, 1960), 537–554.
[52] Vivienne Koch, *William Carlos Williams,* "The Makers of Modern Literature" (Norfolk, Connecticut: New Directions Books, 1950), 36.

Art very possibly *ought* to be the supreme achievement, the "accomplished" but there is the other satisfactory effect, that of a man hurling himself at an indomitable chaos, and yanking and hauling as much of it as possible into some sort of order (or beauty), aware of it both as chaos and potential.[53]

This was Williams' achievement in *Paterson*, to show us

> rolling up out of chaos,
> a nine months' wonder, the city.

---

[53] Quoted in Louis Martz, "Recent Poetry," *Yale Review,* XXXVIII (September, 1948), 148.